GEORGE PAPADOGEORGOS

PROMINENT GREEKS
OF ANTIQUITY
THEIR LIVES AND WORK

EDITIONS
TOUBI'S
ΕΚΔΟΣΕΙΣ

© Copyright   MICHAEL TOUBIS PUBLICATIONS S.A.
                  Nisiza Karela, Koropi, Attica, Greece.
                  Telephone: +30 210 6029974
                  Fax: +30 210 6646856
                  Web Site: http://www.toubis.gr

ISBN: 960-540-465-6

*T*his book is dedicated to the ancient Hellenic spirit.
The thought of Greek philosophers, the works of artists,
the vision of politicians, the words of orators and, above
all, the writings of historians who tried to convey us to
the climate of ancient Greek thought – all constitute
significant landmarks to which the scholarly community
can refer as well as the ordinary man or woman
in search of substance. In an age where we are literally
inundated with information, ancient Greek thought
is of interest since, free of needless euphemisms,
it is always timely and essential. It is a luminous milestone
in any voyage of the mind.
In this book one can find information about the life
and works of the most significant representatives
of the ancient Hellenic spirit – although when
we are discussing a very broad intellectual horizon,
the "significant" is necessarily dictated by the
subjectivity of publication needs. Their maxims
and aphorisms that were respected by every
development in the Greek language and excerpts
from their works accompanied by a wealth of
photographic material transform this book into a point of
departure for a voyage toward the world of wisdom.

CONTENTS

POLITICIANS, ORATORS, WRITERS... THE WORDSMITHS

PHILOSOPHERS

I. THE PRE-SOCRATIC PHILOSOPHERS

The philosophers whose work constituted the intellectual foundation that paved the way for Socrates.

A. The Seven Wise Men of Antiquity

They lived in Greece in the 6th century BC and became famous for their social or political wisdom and prudence. (Thales of Miletus, Pittacus of Mytilene, Solon of Athens, Bias of Priene, Cleobulus of Rhodes, Chilon of Sparta, Periander of Corinth).

B. The Ionian School

They regarded the world as a succession of alterations in existing perceptible matter. (Anaximander of Miletus, Heraclitus of Ephesus, Leucippus of Miletus, Democratis of Abdera, Anaximenes of Miletus).

E. The Sophists

They gathered with others in Athens in the second half of the 5th century BC and gave lessons in rhetoric and politics, for a fee. (Protagoras of Abdera, Gorgias of Leontini).

D. The Pythagoreans

There were various degrees of initiation in this school. Strict discipline prevailed among the pupils. Secret and mysterious rituals covered the teachings while the pupils were not entitled either to write or to disseminate orally what they were taught. (Pythagoras of Samos, Archytas of Tarentum).

C. The Eleatic School

Its representatives came from Elea in Lower Italy (from which the philosophical school took its name) and believed that everything is one being, since it resides in all beings. (Parmenides of Elea, Zeno of Elea).

II. SOCRATES

Perhaps the greatest philosopher of all times. Came from Athens and studied concepts and moral problems through dialectics, a method of searching for the truth with questions and answers.

III. THE SCHOOL OF PLATO

Developed the theory of ideas. (Plato, Xenocrates of Chalcedon).

IV. ARISTOTLE AND THE PERIPATETICS

Aristotle and his pupils were called *Peripatetics* owing to the walks (*peripatoi*) they took together with their teacher in the gardens of the Lyceum where he taught.

V. PLOTINOS AND THE NEOPLATONISTS

Plotinus was the main representative of Neoplatonic School that linked Platonic doctrines with Eastern and Judaic teachings, and believed the primary principle to be union with the divine through purifyi asceticism.

VI. STOIC PHILOSOPHY

The Stoics believed that man achieves his purpose, which is happiness, through a life in which all desires are subjugated to virtue, a life in conformity to the power that governs the world, i.e. reason, universal logic; they attached particular significance to the satisfaction of natural desires. (Chrysippus of Cilicia, Poseidonius of Apamea or Rhodes)

VII. DIOGENES AND THE CYNICS

Diogenes was the founder of a school of philosophy that taught that man's limitation of his needs, his independence from the world around him and even from himself bring him close to the divine.

VIII. EPICURUS OF SAMOS

Representative of a school of philosophy according to which philosophy and knowledge serve happiness, while the only absolute good is pleasure (not of the moment but long-term) and the only absolute evil is pain.

ARTISTS

I. POETRY

A. Epic poetry
Poems with a heroic subject in which the themes are mainly taken from the great wars, and from the misfortunes and triumphs of a people.
(Homer, Hesiod)

B. Lyric poetry
Lyric poetry was sung in antiquity to the accompaniment of music in general and the lyre in particular. Today the same term is used to describe poetry that expresses feelings and the inner world of the poet directly and subjectively.
(Archilochus of Paros, Sappho, Alcaeus, Alcman, Pindar, Bacchylides of Ceos, Anacreon).

C. Idylls
A poetic genre that flourished in the Hellenistic period. The Idylls are brief descriptive poems or dialogues of exceptional skill on subjects from rural, mainly pastoral life written in a tender and erotic tone.
(Theocritus).

D. Alexandrians
The poets bearing this name are from the period extending from the death of Alexander the Great (323 BC) to 240 BC.
(Calimachus).

E. Tragedy
Tragedy is a form of solemn drama in which the hero suffers and often dies in such a way as to lead the spectator to psychological "catharsis". As a genre it was born of religious songs that were sung by the chorus during the feasts of Dionysus.
(Aeschylus, Sophocles, Euripides).

F. Comedy
Theatrical works that create mirth by satirising characters, social manners and political life. Ancient comedy arose from the Dionysiac feasts and specifically from the vulgar songs addressed by one to another during the feasts. It developed mainly in Athens.
(Aristophanes, Menander)

II. SCULPTURE
(Phidias, Polyclitus, Paeonius, Praxiteles, Scopas, Lysippus).

III. PAINTING
(Zeuxis or Zeuxippus, Polygnotus).

POLITICIANS - ORATORS - WRITERS

I. POLITICIANS
(Aristides the Just, Themistocles, Cimon, Miltiades, Pericles, Alexander the Great).

II. ORATORS
(Lysias, Aeschines, Demosthenes, Lycurgus, Isocrates).

III. HISTORIANS – WRITERS
(Aesop, Archimedes, Herodotus, Pausanias, Thucydides, Xenophon, Plutarch, Polybius, Arrian, Lucian, Diogenes Laertius).

The School of Athens, *Raphael (1511), fresco in the Room of the Signatura, Vatican.*

PHILOSOPHERS
...LOVERS OF WISDOM

*T*he first section of this book features ancient Greek philosophy starting from the Pre-Socratics:

▸ The seven wise men of antiquity who lived on Greek territories in the 6th century BC and became known for their social or political wisdom and prudence (Thales of Miletus, Pittacus of Mytilene, Solon of Athens, Bias of Priene, Cleobulus of Rhodes, Chilon of Sparta and Periander of Corinth).

▸ The most significant representatives of the Ionian or Physical school who regarded the world as a successive series of alterations of existing perceptible matter (Anaximander of Miletus, Heraclitus of Ephesus, Leucippus of Miletus, Democritus of Abdera, Anaximenes of Miletus).

▸ The founders of the Eleatic school, Parmenides and Zeno, who came from Elea in Lower Italy (from which the philosophical school took its name).

▸ Pythagoras of Samos and his pupil Archytas of Tarentum in Southern Italy who founded the Pythagorean or Italian School in which there were various degrees of initiation.

▸ The Sophists Protagoras of Abdera and Gorgias of Leontini, together with others, who gathered in Athens in the second half of the 5th century BC and gave lessons in rhetoric and politics, for a fee.

Then follows Socrates who was perhaps the greatest philosopher of all times. He was an Athenian and studied concepts and moral problems using dialectics, a method of discovering truth through questions and answers.
After Socrates Plato and Xenocrates are presented. Plato was influenced by Socrates (he was a devoted pupil of his). Plato developed the theory of ideas. His teachings were pursued by his pupil Xenocrates.
Socrates and Plato were followed by:

▸ Aristotle and his pupils who were called Peripatetics owing to the walks (*peripatoi*) they took together with their teacher in the gardens of the Lyceum where he taught.

▸ Plotinus who was the main representative of Neoplatonic school that linked Platonic doctrines with Eastern and Judaic teachings and believed its primary principle to be union with the divine through purifying asceticism.

▸ The Stoics Chrysippus of Cilicia and Poseidonius of Apamea on Syria who believed that man's purpose, happiness, must be achieved through a life in which all desires are subjugated to virtue.

▸ Diogenes the Cynic, the founder of a school of philosophy that taught man to limit his needs.

▸ Epicurus, representative of a school of philosophy according to which only absolute good is pleasure and the only absolute evil is pain.

Baalbeck Mosaic, 3rd cent. AD, that depicted the seven (according to one version) wise men of antiquity grouped around the muse Calliope. Beirut Museum.

THALES OF MILETUS

624-549 BC

Regarded as being the founder of the Ionian School of philosophy, Thales was the first to renounce the religious and mythological explanations of the world and its phenomena that had prevailed up to that time by declaring water to be the elementary cosmic substance out of which all others are formed.

ΑΣΦΑΛΕΣ ΤΟ ΓΕΝΟΜΕΝΟΝ
ΑΣΑΦΕΣ ΤΟ ΜΕΛΛΟΝ

What's done is known.
What's to come is not.

ΤΟΙΣ ΕΠΙΤΗΔΕΙΟΙΣ ΣΥΓΧΡΩ

Seek the company
of capable men.

ΙΣΧΥΡΟΤΑΤΟΝ ΑΝΑΓΚΗ
ΚΡΑΤΕΙ ΓΑΡ ΠΑΝΤΩΝ

Necessity is most powerful
for it subjugates everything.

ΦΘΟΝΟΥ ΜΑΛΛΟΝ
Η ΟΙΚΤΙΡΟΥ

Better to be envied
than pitied.

ΣΟΦΩΤΑΤΟΣ ΧΡΟΝΟΣ
ΑΝΕΥΡΙΣΚΕΙ ΓΑΡ ΠΑΝΤΑ

Wise time discovers all.

ΧΑΛΕΠΟΝ ΕΑΥΤΟΝ ΓΝΩΝΑΙ

It is difficult to know yourself.

His life and work

Thales believed that matter, of which the universe is made, is subject to constant changes that are brought about by the gods, powerful beings inherent in every particle of matter. He also sought a single elementary cosmic matter as the base of the diversity of nature, and declared this to be water.

Most of the information we have about the life and work of Thales of Miletus is from the writings of the ancient Greek historian Diogenes Laertius. The appellation «Wise Man» (*Sophos*) initially applied to Thales and six other Greek men was derived from a term that then designated inventiveness and practical wisdom rather than speculative insight.

Thales is said to have had extensive knowledge of mathematics, astronomy and physics. To him we owe a number of theorems in geometry such as that opposite angles are equal when two straight lines intersect, that the angles at the base of an isosceles triangle are equal, that the angle inscribed in a semicircle is a right angle, and others.

Thales was also an important astronomer. According to Eudemus of Rhodes, in his *History of Astronomy,* Thales was the first to speak of eclipses of the sun and established the solstices. Herodotus reported that Thales predicted the solar eclipse of 585 BC, when a battle was taking place between the Lydians and the Persians. Thales likewise had some knowledge of mechanics. To enable Croesus's army to cross the River Halys, wrote Herodotus, Thales shifted the bed of the river in such a way that Croesus' army was on the other side. Thales was the first known scientist in the world in the full sense of the word. The ancient Greeks believed that it was Thales who introduced geometry into the Aegean world. He won the profound esteem of his contemporaries for his sagacity.

An epigram was carved on his tomb in Miletus that began with a phrase:

«ὀλίγον τόδε σῆμα, τό δέ κλέος οὐρανόμηκες»
meaning:
"This grave may be small, but its glory reaches heaven".

Ο ΜΕΛΛΕΙΣ ΠΟΙΕΙΝ ΜΗ ΛΕΓΕ, ΑΠΟΤΥΧΩΝ ΓΑΡ ΚΑΤΑΓΕΛΑΣΘΗΣΗΣ

Speak not about what you will do in the future;
for if you fail you will be ridiculed.

PITTACUS
OF MYTILENE (IN LESBOS)

648-569 BC

He was a model of prudence
and a political figure distinguished for his
reason, wisdom and political honesty.
He granted freedom even to the
murderer of his son, arguing that
«forgiveness is better than regret».
His considerable political abilities are
confirmed by a number of laws including
the one that stipulated a double penalty for
any offence committed while intoxicated.

ΦΟΒΟΥ ΤΑ ΑΙΣΧΡΑ
Beware of the unethical.

ΑΡΧΗ ΑΝΔΡΑ ΔΕΙΚΝΥΣΙ
Power reveals the man.

ΜΗ ΤΗΝ ΟΨΙΝ ΚΑΛΛΩΠΙΖΟΥ ΑΛΛ ΕΝ ΤΟΙΣ ΕΠΙΤΗΔΕΥΜΑΣΙΝ ΙΣΘΙ ΚΑΛΟΣ
Do not beautify your appearance,
but in your works be good.

ΜΗ ΠΛΟΥΤΕΙ ΚΑΚΩΣ
Do not become rich unjustly.

ΑΝΙΑΡΟΝ ΑΡΓΙΑ
Idleness is distressing.

ΚΑΙΡΟΝ ΓΝΩΘΙ
Know when to act.

ΜΗΔΕΝΑ ΠΡΟ ΤΟΥ ΤΕΛΟΥΣ ΜΑΚΑΡΙΖΕ
Call no man fortunate until he dies.

His life

Pittacus probably came from an aristocratic family, since his mother was a noble-woman from the island of Lesbos and his father was from the middle or upper classes of Thrace. Other information, originating mainly from his political adversaries, indicated that Pittacus was of humble origin, and that he spent his childhood unhappily and humbly, but being the very intelligent and active person he was, he managed to over-come all difficulties and hurdles created by his humble origin.

He was self-educated and travelled widely. With his intelligence, prudence and political honesty, and his wisdom and courage in battle, he played a very important role in the history of his country. In 589 his fellow citizens elected him *Aisymnetes*, entrusting him with absolute power in times of internal strife.

His work

Pittacus was involved in politics and governed Mytilene prudently for 10 years. According to Diogenes Laertius, when the Athenians attacked Mytilene, its inhabitants had Pittacus as their general. He challenged the Athenian general Phrynon to a duel and defeated him, which made his fellow citizens recognise his services and allow him to govern Mytilene. He is reported to have ruled in a spirit of justice, seeking to calm political passions. He showed sympathy to all political factions by proclaiming a general amnesty. He was the first to give the example of tolerance, granting freedom to the murderer of his own son, stating that *"forgiveness is better than repentance"*.

He enacted new laws and took care to foster trade and to emancipate the people. It is reported that one of his best laws was the one that provided for a double punishment for any offence that had been committed when the offender was drunk. When he felt he had completed his political programme, he retired from office of his own volition and lived the remaining ten years of his life as an ordinary citizen.

His political sagacity and moral stature were recognised very soon.

Diogenes Laertius quotes a number of moral and political maxims attributed to him, as well as an undoubtedly spurious letter he is reported to have written to Croesus - who had allegedly sent him a lavish gift of money - telling him that he always had twice as much as he needed.

A number of other writers of antiquity also attributed maxims to him.

Pittacus wrote six hundred lines of elegiac poetry, as well as a prose text containing laws for the citizens. His poetry was admonitory in nature and, taken as a whole, con-stituted an account of his political action.

He lived more than seventy years. The following epigram was carved on his grave:

> *"With the appropriate tears, sacred Lesbos mourns*
> *for Pittacus whom it produced and now is dead".*

ΑΡΧΕΣΘΑΙ ΜΑΘΩΝ ΑΡΧΕΙΝ ΕΠΙΣΤΗΣΕΙ

Learn to be ruled
that you may rule.

ΣΥΜΒΟΥΛΕΥΕ ΜΗ ΤΑ ΗΔΙΣΤΑ ΑΛΛΑ ΤΑ ΑΡΙΣΤΑ

Do not advise the pleasant
but the proper.

ΗΔΟΝΗΝ ΦΕΥΓΕ ΗΤΙΣ ΥΣΤΕΡΟΝ ΛΥΠΗΝ ΤΙΚΤΕΙ

Avoid pleasure,
which then brings sadness.

SOLON OF ATHENS

640-558 BC

Solon's law regarding apathetic citizens

Of all Solon's laws, the most characteristic and strange is the law stipulating that in the event
of civil unrest in the city, every man had to side with a faction, otherwise he would lose his
civil rights. It seems that Solon did not want a single citizen to be indifferent to public issues,
or to seek only his own interests, or to take pride in the fact that the sufferings of his
homeland cause him no pain. On the contrary, Solon wanted the citizen to take a position
at the outset alongside those he believed to be acting most correctly and justly,
and to take a risk and help them instead of waiting safely to see who would win.

(Plutarch, Solon, **20)**

ΓΗΡΑΣΚΩ Δ'ΑΕΙ ΠΟΛΛΑ ΔΙΔΑΣΚΟΜΕΝΟΣ

The older I become the more I learn.

His life

Poet, legislator and philosopher, Solon came from a noble family, and as a young man, maintained himself as a merchant. He travelled far and wide on his own ship, educating himself and making money. But he considered earthly goods in the right light: he believed that people who have *"piles of gold and silver, fruitful fields, horses and mules"* were as happy as those who have *"nothing but their health -a strong stomach, a strong body and legs- and when the time comes, a pretty wife. Thus their happiness is complete".*

But this wise man did not disdain the joys of life: "The works of Dionysus and the Muses, a source of delight to men, this is what I like!"

His work

In 594 BC, in recognition of his services in recapturing the island of Salamis from the Megarians, the Athenians elected Solon to the position of Archon with unlimited powers and with a mandate to exercise economic and social reforms. Because the land was concentrated in the hands of a few, the poorer classes kept multiplying and falling deeper in debt, and discontent was rife in the state. Solon undertook this high mission and succeeded in instituting laws and establishing social measures that constituted a historic landmark in the city of Athens, creating the conditions necessary for its subsequent glory.

Among the measures he took were:

- to abolish debts through the *Seisachtheia* ("shaking off burdens"), a law that cancelled loans granted on the property or person of the borrower. He then set free people whose debts had reduced them to slavery.
- to lay down a new basis for distinguishing citizens into four classes with different rights: the wealthy Pentacosiomedimni, the horsemen Hippeis, the Zeugites who tilled the land, and the Thetes who were servants, artisans, etc., according to each one's property and income rather than his family origin, as had been the case hitherto.
- to prohibit the export of cereals from Attica, since it could not feed its own people, although he permitted the export of oil which was abundant.
- to take economic measures to bridge the gap between the aristocracy and the lower social classes.
- to encourage the settlement of *metoikoi* (emigrants).
- to grant the right by law to those who had no descendants to dispose of their property as they wished, i.e. the division of family lands.
- to make provision by law to oblige citizens to adhere to one or the other faction in a civil dispute under penalty of losing their rights.
- to grant amnesty to all exiled Athenians.
- to pass a law allowing any citizen to bring charges against another who damaged the honour, life and property of a third citizen.

In his mature poetry he called upon his fellow citizens to take bold actions, emphasising their patriotism.

BIAS OF PRIENE
6th century BC

ΝΟΣΟΝ ΨΥΧΗΣ ΤΟ ΤΩΝ
ΑΔΥΝΑΤΩΝ ΕΡΑΝ

To desire the impossible
is a sickness of the mind.

ΕΦΟΔΙΟΝ ΑΠΟ ΝΕΟΤΗΤΟΣ ΕΙΣ
ΓΗΡΑΣ ΑΝΑΛΑΜΒΑΝΕ ΣΟΦΙΑΝ
ΒΕΒΑΙΟΤΕΡΟΝ ΓΑΡ ΤΟΥΤΟ
ΤΩΝ ΑΛΛΩΝ ΚΤΗΜΑΤΩΝ

Provide yourself with wisdom
from youth to old age,
because it is a more lasting
possession than anything else.

His life and work

Bias was born in Priene, a town north of Miletus in Ionia, Asia Minor, which maintained links with Thebes. In it the main sanctuary of the Ionians was located.

He was renowned for his wisdom, his flawless judicial judgement and his eloquence. He defended in court those who had been unjustly treated, and indeed without fee. When he was obliged to sentence someone to death, he would weep. It is said that when Alyattes, king of Lydia, laid siege to Priene, Bias let loose two well-fed mules into Alyattes' camp. The latter, seeing the mules, was astonished at their excellent condition and concluded that for livestock to be so well fed, the inhabitants must be living under very good conditions. To verify this, he sent a messenger into the city. Then Bias ordered piles of sand to be created, and wheat to be poured on top of them, which he then showed to the emissary. When Alyapes learned about this, he sought peace with Priene. Bias died at the age of 80 as he was speaking in the court. He was honoured by a splendid funeral and a sanctuary called Teutaminum was dedicated to him.

ΠΕΙΣΑΣ ΛΑΒΕ ΜΗ ΒΙΑΣΑΜΕΝΟΣ
Take by persuasion not force.

CLEOBULUS OF RHODES

6th century BC

*Cleobulus of Rhodes. Detail from the Baalbeck mosaic.
Beirut Museum. 3rd century AD.*

ΓΛΩΤΤΗΣ ΚΡΑΤΕΙΝ

Hold your tongue.

ΒΙΑ ΜΗΔΕΝ ΠΡΑΤΤΕΙΝ

Do nothing by force.

ΕΥΤΥΧΩΝ ΜΗ ΙΣΘΙ
ΥΠΕΡΗΦΑΝΟΣ ΑΠΟΡΗΣΑΣ
ΜΗ ΤΑΠΕΙΝΟΥ

Show not pride when wealthy,
nor undue servility when poor.

His life and work

Cleobulus was the tyrant (a word which in antiquity meant absolute ruler) of Rhodes (Lindos) and one of the seven sages of ancient Greece. He lived in the 6th century BC, but we do not know exactly when he was born or when he died. His father boasted that his family was descended from Hercules. He was distinguished for his physical strength and handsome appearance. He had travelled widely and was well acquainted with Egyptian philosophy. He wrote poetry, riddles and epigrams. He had a daughter, Cleobuline, who was a writer of riddles and hexameter poems. Cleobuline was discussed by Cratinus in his work entitled *Cleobulinae*.

Cleobulus refurbished the sanctuary of Athena that had been built by Danaus.

Of all the riddles for which Cleobulus was famed, only a few have survived including this one, the answer to which is time:

> *"The father is one and his children twelve.*
> *Each of the children has twice thirty daughters*
> *who have a different appearance.*
> *Some are white others black some are immortal while others die".*

ΜΕΤΡΟΝ ΑΡΙΣΤΟΝ

Measure in all things.

ΜΗ ΠΡΟΤΡΕΧΕΤΩ
Η ΓΛΩΤΤΑ ΤΗΣ ΔΙΑΝΟΙΑΣ

Think before you speak.

ΤΑΧΥΤΕΡΟΝ ΕΠΙ ΤΑΣ
ΑΤΥΧΙΑΣ ΤΩΝ ΦΙΛΩΝ
Η ΕΠΙ ΤΑΣ ΕΥΤΥΧΙΑΣ
ΠΟΡΕΥΕΣΘΑΙ

Tread more rapidly through
the misfortunes of your friends
than through their good fortune.

CHILON
OF SPARTA

6th century BC

His life and work

Chilon lived in the 6th century BC. He was the son of Damagetus and his family was from Sparta (Lacedaemon). What ranked Chilon among the Seven Sages was his reform of the institutions established by Lycurgus; on the basis of this reform, power was given to the *ephors*. Under the laws of Lycurgus, the ephors were mere assistants to the two *basileis* (or kings), without any particular political role. But Chilon, cleverly taking ad-vantage of the current situation, had the *ephors* made deputies of the basileis when the latter were absent, or when the kingdom was "lame", i.e. when one of the two basileis could not exercise power, or when they disagreed about something.

Chilon wrote about two hundred elegiac verses and said that the great virtue of man was prudence and well-grounded judgement as to future events. The characteristic feature of Chilon was the laconic way in which he expressed his philosophical convic-tions. He believed the most difficult things for man to do were to keep secrets, to control his nerves and to suffer injustice.

Tradition tells us that Chilon died of great joy when he heard that his son had won a contest in the Olympic Games. The inscription on his tomb concludes with the words: *"We too would be fortunate to have such a death"*.

PERIANDER OF CORINTH

668-584 BC

ΜΗΔΕΝ ΧΡΗΜΑΤΩΝ
ΕΝΕΚΑ ΠΡΑΤΤΕΙΝ

Do nothing for the sake of money.

ΕΠΙΣΦΑΛΕΣ ΠΡΟΠΕΤΕΙΑ

Rashness is dangerous.

Ο ΑΝ ΟΜΟΛΟΓΗΣΕΙΣ ΔΙΑΤΗΡΕΙ

When you give your word, keep it.

ΜΕΛΕΤΗ ΤΟ ΠΑΝ

Attention is everything.

His life and work

Periander was tyrant of Corinth for 40 years. He succeeded the tyranny of his father Cypselus. To consolidate his power, he did not hesitate to commit the most heinous crimes. It is said, for example, that in a moment of anger, he killed his own wife, thus coming into conflict with his father-in-law, Proclus, tyrant of Epidaurus, whose territory he eventually seized. It is also possible that his reputation as a cruel despot may have stemmed largely from the Corinthian nobility whom he treated harshly.

What is certain is that Periander, though his firm and effective rule, became famous as the founder of Corinthian greatness. He worked hard to increase its power and prosperity. He enacted brilliant measures to protect and promote Corinthian trade, making it the major maritime power of the age. Under his rule, Corinth reached the height of its political power, established the colonies of Apollonia, Epidaumnus and Potidaea, and annexed Corfu. From the economic point of view, under Periander's rule, Corinth was the most important city in Greece, with its industry and trade reaching unprecedented heights. Periander restricted luxury and prohibited the purchase of slaves. He also introduced drastic legislation against idleness, luxury and vice. He took care to develop shipping. He even thought of cutting through the isthmus of Corinth, but was obliged to abandon this plan owing to the lack of engineering resources. Periander, patron of poets and artists, is reputed to have been the author of a collection of maxims in 2000 verses.

Statue of a philosopher. Delphi Museum.

ANAXIMANDER OF MILETUS

610-547 BC

His life and work

He was a philosopher from Miletus and contemporary of Thales. He too is reported to have travelled widely through the Black Sea, the Aegean Islands, mainland Greece, and to Egypt and Babylon.

He came from a wealthy family and, like Thales, studied astronomy and mathematics. He also built a solar clock as well as a heavenly sphere and drew a map of the earth. In the field of science, he continued the work of Thales, whose pupil he had been. Unfortunately, his work *On Nature*, which as far as we know is the most ancient work written in prose, was lost. Just one phrase has been preserved which capsulated his view of the infinite and the way in which he understood it. As Theophrastus* informs us, Anaximander called matter infinite. By this term he meant the matter that is totally unrelated to air, water and the other elements, i.e. amorphous matter from which all things and the world in general were made. The infinite, according to Anaximander, is an endless, unlimited mass; it cannot be lost, it has no end. There are collisions and changes of elements in nature, but nothing is lost. Whatever is lost today will emerge again tomorrow. The infinite is incorruptible.

Anaximander was also the first man in recorded history to use the term "principle", a term that has since then become common in philosophy. Regarding the Earth, Anaximander believed that it was formed by the condensation of the liquid element that existed initially, that it is cylindrical in shape and immobile at the centre of the universe.

Anaximander attributed the generation of life to the liquid element, through the action of heat from the sun. With his view of the origin of man from an aquatic life form, Anaximander introduced the idea of evolution in biology.

As an astronomer, physicist, biologist and philosopher, Anaximander was a innovator, and a large number of the philosophical problems of subsequent centuries, up to the modern age, were inherent in his philosophical system.

---

*Theophrastus: philosopher from Eresus, Lesbos, associate and successor of Aristotle, 4-3rd century BC.

HERACLITUS OF EPHESUS

6th century BC

**Heraclitus is regarded
as one of the most important
of the pre-Socratic philosophers.
For Heraclitus, birth is a product of
the struggle between the elements, fire,
and war. Life emerges solely from fire.**

ΚΑΙ ΕΚ ΠΑΝΤΩΝ ΕΝ ΚΑΙ
ΕΞ ΕΝΟΣ ΠΑΝΤΑ

Reality is both one and many.

ΚΑΚΟΙ ΜΑΡΤΥΡΕΣ
ΑΝΘΡΩΠΟΙΣΙ ΟΦΘΑΛΜΟΙ
ΚΑΙ ΩΤΑ ΒΑΡΒΑΡΟΥΣ
ΨΥΧΑΣ ΕΧΟΝΤΩΝ

The senses are bad witnesses;
only the wise man
can obtain knowledge.

ΗΛΙΟΣ ΟΥΧ
ΥΠΕΡΒΗΣΕΤΑΙ ΜΕΤΡΑ

The road up and the road down
are one and the same.

ΠΟΛΕΜΟΣ ΠΑΝΤΩΝ
ΜΕΝ ΠΑΤΗΡ,
ΠΑΝΤΩΝ ΔΕ ΒΑΣΙΛΕΥΣ

War is the father of all things.

ΠΟΤΑΜΩ ΓΑΡ ΟΥΚ ΕΣΤΙΝ
ΕΜΒΗΝΑΙ ΔΙΣ ΤΩ ΑΥΤΩ

You cannot swim twice
in the same river.

ΠΑΝΤΑ ΡΕΙ, ΕΙΝΑΙ ΔΕ ΠΑΓΙΩΣ ΟΥΔΕΝ

All is flux, nothing stays still.

His life

We know little about Heraclitus's life. He was a melancholy and unsociable man, with contempt for mankind, but with a strong and independent spirit. Since he could see that democracy frequently ended in anarchy,

Heraclitus declined the high position in the city ensured to him by his aristocratic origin, and withdrew entirely from public affairs into the solitude of the famous sanctuary of Artemis (Ephesus).

His work

As a philosopher, he formulated some important and original thoughts. He was one of the first to speak of the change and evolution of beings. He regarded fire, "primeval" and "eternal", as the fundamental component of matter. Fire, which changes, is transformed first into water, and then condenses into earth (soil, rocks) from which it even-tually returns to its initial state, i.e. becoming fire again, in a constant cyclical movement.

Heraclitus formulated his philosophy of evolution, of *Becoming* in his famous maxim *Panta rei* ("All is flux") which means that everything is in a constant state of motion, and in his other famous phrase "You cannot swim twice in the same river".

Heraclitus declared that "All things are, and nothing stays still", i.e. every birth, according to Heraclitus, is a product of those elements of nature that are in constant struggle and opposition. From the struggle of the elements harmony is born. The permanence of things is illusory and is due to the fact that opposing forces are momentarily balanced. Without them, there would be no life. This is why he spoke of the war between the elements as being the father of all things and said that their motive force was *pyr* (fire). More heat meant more motion and awareness. More cold meant immobility, stillness. In his work *On Nature* he did not follow the method of analysis and proof, for he did not consider that the reader might have objections or difficulties, but wrote in the style of aphorisms, with a wealth of illustrations and pithy maxims, that frequently bring to mind the prophecies of an oracle. This is why, for many people Heraclitus was the "dark" philosopher.

Diogenes Laertius reported that Euripides gave Heraclitus's work to Socrates, and when the latter had read it, Euripides asked him: *"What did you think of it?"*

Socrates replied: *"What I understood is important; but I think that what I could not understand was equally important; you have to be a very strong swimmer of the spirit not to drown in his book".*

Heraclitus, although we do not have his teaching in its entirety, is the most important of the pre-Socratic philosophers. He had a very broad mind and his philosophy on many basic points constitutes an original view of the world. He is a dialectical but simple materialist. For this reason, his philosophy exerted great influence not only in antiquity, but primarily in modern times, in the philosophy of Hegel and in the general formulation of dialectical concepts.

LEUCIPPUS OF MILETUS

5th century BC

Perhaps Leucippus's most important contribution
to philosophy was his recognition that the true identity
of every object comes only from genuine mathematical
concepts the violation of which can cause changes
to the cosmic system. The notion of causality
was introduced into philosophical thought
for the first time by the views of Leucippus.

ΠΑΝΤΑ ΚΑΤ'ΑΝΑΓΚΗΝ ΤΗΝ Δ'ΑΥΤΗΝ ΥΠΑΡΧΕΙΝ ΕΙΜΑΡΜΕΝΗΝ

All things are moved by some necessity, in which is destiny.

His life

Philosopher of the 5th century BC. His very existence was disputed even by Epicurus, who is regarded as continuing the atomistic theory. The precise period during which he was active is not known, but we do know that he was a contemporary of Empedocles and Anaxagoras. In all likelihood, he came from Miletus, although tradition places his homeland in either Elea (southern Italy) or Abdera (Thrace). In any event, in 450/449 he went to Elea where he became a pupil of Zeno and from there he travelled to Abdera, where he settled permanently and founded his school.

This School has remained in history with the title Atomistic Philosophy because it investigated the composition of matter, on different criteria of course. Its founders were Leucippus and Democritus, but its precursor was Anaxagoras.

His work

The work and teachings of Leucippus have not come down to us in their original form, because they were merged with the work of Democritus, which must be regarded as the product of the collaboration between these two top-ranking atomist philosophers. Despite this, two works believed to have been written by Leucippus are The *Great World System* in which he analysed the physical basis of the atomist theory, explaining the creation and structure of the world, and *On the mind* which contained his teaching about the operation of the senses and images. From the second work, the following phrase has been preserved:

«Οὐδέν χρῆμα μάτην γίγνεται,
ἀλλά πάντα ἐκ λόγου τε καί ὑπ' ἀνάγκης».

meaning:

*"Nothing is accidental,
all things happen for some reason
or necessity".*

The philosophy of Leucippus, which is based on the ideas of Parmenides, introduced two opposing concepts: the full, which represents *being* and the void which is equivalent to *non-being*. An attribute of the former concept is infinite smallness, with the logical implication of indivisibility, which for this reason is called *atomos* (i.e. indivisible).

The order observed in the universe is for Leucippus a result of the inviolable appli-cation of laws determining the flow and whirling of atoms.

The senses, which lead to the perception of the world, have as a starting point the intermingling of atoms, which according to shape, class or position create the imp-ression of attributes.

DEMOCRITUS OF ABDERA (THRACE)

470 or 460 BC-361 or 360 BC

According to the theory
formulated by Democritus,
being is as existent as non-being.
Material is indivisible and is comprised of
an invisible part, the atom, which cannot
be divided. Many atoms exist which are
interconnected in various ways,
obeying purely mechanical laws
and forming miscellaneous beings
that are known to us. Even though his
theory about the indivisibility of the atom
has today been disproved,
Democritus's notion of the universe
laid the foundation
for progress in scientific research.

ΟΜΟΦΡΟΣΥΝΗ
ΦΙΛΙΗΝ ΠΟΕΙ

Similarity creates friendship.

ΕΙ ΤΙΣ ΥΠΕΡΒΑΛΛΟΙ
ΤΟ ΜΕΤΡΙΟΝ,
ΤΑ ΕΠΙΤΕΡΠΕΣΤΑΤΑ
ΑΤΕΡΠΑΣΤΑ ΑΝ ΓΙΝΟΙΤΟ

Even the most pleasant
becomes unpleasant in excess.

Ο ΚΟΣΜΟΣ ΣΚΗΝΗ,
Ο ΒΙΟΣ ΠΑΡΟΔΟΣ.
ΗΛΘΕΣ, ΕΙΔΕΣ, ΑΠΗΛΘΕΣ

The world is a stage, life a passage.
You came, you saw, you left.

ΠΑΤΡΟΣ ΣΩΦΡΟΣΥΝΗ
ΜΕΓΙΣΤΟΝ ΤΕΚΝΟΙΣ
ΠΑΡΑΓΓΕΛΜΑ

The father's temperance
is the child's great legacy.

ΝΙΚΑΝ ΑΥΤΟΝ ΕΑΥΤΟΝ
ΠΑΣΩΝ ΝΙΚΩΝ
ΠΡΩΤΗ ΚΑΙ ΑΡΙΣΤΗ

Victory over self is the first
and greatest victory.

His life

Most of the information we have about the life of Democritus agrees that he was sufficiently well off to be able to travel widely in the East. He went to Miletus, where he received his early education in philosophy, and then to Asia to study astronomy from the original sources, and to learn the natural sciences from the Egyptians, the Chaldeans and the Persians. He also journeyed to India where he became acquainted with the "Naked philosophers", or ascetics of India. At the end, he returned to Athens impoverished, but rich in experience. Tradition tells us that he was called the "laughing philosopher".

His work

The work of Democritus included sixty titles, as recorded by Diogenes Laertius. We can see in the latter's writings that Democritus, a man of wide-ranging spirit, was interested not only in philosophy, but also in philology and the history of literature, music and the physical sciences. He also took up the anatomy of animals. Both Cicero and Plutarch regarded Democritus' prose as worthy of a great author and Dionysus of Alicarnassus did not hesitate to compare his style with that of Plato.

In his teaching, Democritus accepts that non-being is as real as being. Being is indivisible matter, the atom (that which cannot be split), although it is not one but many. Atoms move and become interwoven among themselves to form the various objects and beings we know. This motion obeys purely mechanical laws, with no principle of utility. The various possible encounters of the atoms are: simple contact, collisions, repulsions or adhesions as well as spiral whirling from which bodies result. Some of the conclusions drawn by Democritus from this fundamental theory appear naïve: for example, the senses of hearing and sight are due to emanations thrown off the surface of objects which reach our ears and eyes when multiplied. But a more scientific investigation recognises in these conclusions the basis for subsequent theories of sound and light waves.

ΒΙΟΣ ΑΝΕΟΡΤΑΣΤΟΣ
ΜΑΚΡΑ ΟΔΟΣ ΑΠΑΝΔΟΚΕΥΤΟΣ

Life without celebrations is a long road without inns.

ANAXIMENES OF MILETUS

550-480 BC

His life and work

Chronologically the third in the series of wise men from Mile-tus, after Thales and Anaximan-der, is Anaximenes, a philoso-pher who contributed significan-tly to Greek thought. He was a fellow student and successor to Anaximander in representing Miletus.

Very little information about his life has come down to us. Un-fortunately, of all his writings just one small fragment has survived, and thus our knowledge of his world theory is derived from a secondary source of questio-nable reliability. Everything we know about his teachings has been taken from a special trea-tise by Theophrastus.

Thus, from the little we have of his own works and from other sources, we know that Anaxime-nes regarded air as the underlying substance of beings, as the principle of the mate-

The sundial of Conion,
2nd cent. BC. Archaeological Museum of Tinos.

rial world and its motion. Air is the fundamental substance of the world with attributes that are closer to Thales' water than to Anaximander's infinite. Air is the most mobile of all elements; it inheres in everything and thus is present everywhere, a cause of life and the basis for explaining reality. In all beings it exists as a substance and, according to its density, can appear as water, as earth, or as fire and generally can take on a particular form with specific attributes. In the universe, the earth was formed first, which Anaximenes imagined as being wide in shape, with its foundation resting in the depths of the infinite. Vapours rising above the earth became flame and some of the flames became stars, which have the same shape as the earth and float in the air. The moon receives light from the sun and eclipses of the sun and the moon are due to natural causes. Apart from the stars that are visible to us, there are also others that we cannot see and that cause eclipses of the moon.

The Eleatic School owed its name to the city of Elea in Lower Italy, birthplace of Parmenides and Zeno.

PARMENIDES OF ELEA

540-450 BC

**Parmenides is the main representative
of Presocratic Philosophy.
His work On Nature argues that movement
is an illusion and that the universe is unique,
continuous and immobile. He also formulated the
principle of contradiction and demonstrated the
possibility of logical proof.**

ΚΡΙΤΗΡΙΟΝ ΤΟΝ ΛΟΓΟΝ
ΤΑΣ ΑΙΣΘΗΣΕΙΣ
ΜΗ ΑΚΡΙΒΕΙΣ ΥΠΑΡΧΕΙΝ

Reason is the criterion because the senses deceive.

His life

Philosopher from Elea, from which the name Eleatic is derived, in southern Italy. Like almost all Greek philosophers, Parmenides was not indifferent to the political life of his country and expressed his opinion in writing on various issues relative to the policies that interested him in particular. He was born of a distinguished family and at the beginning appeared to enjoy politics, but Aminias, a Pythagorean, convinced him to abandon politics and take up scientific research. He did not become a Pythagorean, however, because he followed the teachings of Xenophanes which appealed to him more.

His work

Parmenides was the main founder of Eleatic philosophy. He was a pupil of Xenophanes and teacher of Zeno. Contrary to Heraclitus, Parmenides saw immobility, calm and stability everywhere. The long years of political stability in the city state of Elea may have influenced him in forming his concept of the static and stable nature of being. Plato, in the metaphysical formulation of his theory of ideas, learned a great deal from Parmenides, whom he admired greatly. In fact Plato dedicated one of his famous dialogues to this important philosopher and his theory of *being*. This entity, whose nature Parmenides did not formulate clearly, evolved into the metaphysical and immaterial being which, in Plato's language, was given the name *Idea*. Aristotle fought against the theories of Parmenides and all the Eleatic School.

The only work by Parmenides is believed to have been *On Nature*, an epic poem written in hexameter verses (800 1000 verses), praised by ancient art critics. Many fragments of this work have been preserved in continuous discourse, thanks largely to Simplicius who lived some thousand years after Parmenides and was among the last to see his work intact. The philosopher imagines that he is born in a chariot drawn by vigorous mares –the passions of the soul– and that he arrives outside a city. As guardian of the city Parmenides found Justice who would not allow him to enter. But the daughters of the Sun, i.e. the senses, persuade Justice to allow the poet to enter and to take him before the unnamed goddess. The goddess receives him, benevolent and solemn and addresses the following words to him:

> *"Welcome, young man, you who have come*
> *to my abode accompanied by immortal charioteers*
> *and with the horses bearing you,*
> *because it was not evil destiny that set you to follow this road,*
> *but justice and order.*
> *And you must learn everything,*
> *both the serene heart of the unwavering truth -knowledge-*
> *as well as the false opinions of mortals -the phenomena-*
> *where there is no true certainty."*

Justice promises to initiate him into knowledge and reveals to him the reality of being and the deceptive appearance of the world.

Thus, through the words of the goddess in the first part of his poem, Parmenides presents the theory of being that is identical with perceivable reality, and in the second part the theory of the physical world, as it appears in human experience.

Parmenides introduced a primitive reasoning that precluded beginning and end, birth and death, growth and corruption, movement and change, and the divisibility and the non-continuity of being. He regarded light and night as cosmological principles.

ZENO OF ELEA

5th century BC

ΤΟ ΟΜΟΛΟΓΟΥΜΕΝΩΣ
ΤΗ ΦΥΣΕΙ ΖΗΝ ΟΠΕΡ ΕΣΤΙ
ΚΑΤ'ΑΡΕΤΗΝ ΖΗΝ·
ΑΓΕΙ ΓΑΡ ΠΡΟΣ ΤΑΥΤΗΝ
ΗΜΑΣ Η ΦΥΣΙΣ

Life in agreement with nature
is the same as virtuous life;
because virtue is the end
to which nature leads us.

**Zeno of Elea is regarded as the precursor
of Einstein's theory of relativity.
He was the pupil of Parmenides and 25 years
his junior. In order to support his master's
theory that there were not many beings,
he developed various theories related
to movement, which present a number
of problems.**

ΓΑΜΒΡΟΥ Ο ΜΕΝ
ΕΠΙΤΥΧΩΝ ΕΥΡΕΝ ΥΙΟΝ,
Ο ΔΕ ΑΠΟΤΥΧΩΝ
ΑΠΩΛΕΣΕ ΘΥΓΑΤΕΡΑ

He who has a good son-in-law
has acquired a son;
he who fails in this has lost a daughter.

His life

Zeno of Elea - not to be confused with the Stoic philosopher Zeno of Citium- was born early in the 5th century BC in Elea, Italy, a colony of the Phocaeans. He was a pupil of Parmenides, founder of the Eleatic school of philosophy.

It is also said that he was one of the teachers of Pericles. Tradition has made him a brave political leader who took part in an insurrection against Nearchus, tyrant of Elea, who had him arrested and tortured brutally. Antisthenes reports that during the interrogation, so as not to betray his companions, he bit off his own tongue and spat it in the face of the tyrant. Heraclides reports that he bit off the tyrant's ear, after which the tyrant ordered that he be put to death by being crushed in a mortar.

His work:

Plato and Aristotle preserved a few of Zeno's teachings. Aristotle regarded him as the inventor of dialectics, but in his Physics he rejects Zeno's views of space, time and motion. The following titles of Zeno's works are cited: *Discord, Explanations of Empedocles, To philosophers, On Nature*. He also wrote aphorisms, some of which have been preserved.

Plato often mentions him in his dialogue *Parmenides* and informs us that, when Zeno was in Athens, he always had large audiences, because his theories stimulated the interest of the Athenians and particularly of young people.

In support of Parmenides's theory of Being, Zeno argued that there is neither motion nor multiplicity. The arrow only appears to fly, and swift-footed Achilles never reached the turtle because it is possible, at least in thought, to divide the distance separating them eternally.

Paradoxes of this type demonstrated the unintelligible nature of the Eleatic School. It was a dialectical game, but a serious game, a "playful treatise" according to the Platonic formulation. The paradoxes of Zeno, his "puzzles", were famous. For example, he claimed that every body is infinitely small and, simultaneously, infinitely great: infinitely small, because the parts of which it consists must be indivisible, and therefore without magnitude. And infinitely great since with these endless divisions emerges an infinite number of parts of which the body is made and, since however many are used an infinite number will be left over, the body can grow *ad Infinitum*.

Three other paradoxes concerned the arrow, the bushel and baldness. The flying arrow is motionless because, at any moment in time which he calls the present, it is in just one place. one place. The *medimnos* (unit of volume and measurement) is based on the syllogism that when one grain of corn falls it does not make any noise, whereas when a whole bushel of corn is turned out on the floor, it makes a noise. Therefore the noise that the bushel makes is an illusion, as is the absence of noise when one grain of corn falls.

On the subject of baldness, things are even more complex: *"How many hairs must a head lose to become bald? One hair is responsible for the transition from one state to the other"*. The *paradoxes* are the precursors of the Kant's antinomies; and many people have found in Zeno an embryonic form of the theory of relativity. Zeno is today the most timely pre-Socratic philosopher and is regarded as having exercised a decisive influence on Leucippus and Democritus in formulating the atomist theory, as well as on the Sophists Gorgias and Protagoras. The benefit to science from the theories of Zeno was enormous.

The statue of Pythagoras at the Pythagoreio on Samos.

PYTHAGORAS
OF SAMOS

570-500 BC

ΔΟΥΛΕΥΕΙΝ ΠΑΘΕΣΙ
ΧΑΛΕΠΩΤΕΡΟΝ Η ΤΥΡΑΝΝΟΙΣ

It is worse to be a slave
of the passions than of tyrants.

ΟΥ ΤΑ ΠΑΝΤΑ ΤΟΙΣ ΠΑΣΙ ΡΗΤΑ

You cannot explain
everything to everyone.

ΜΗ ΕΝ ΠΟΛΛΟΙΣ ΟΛΙΓΑ ΛΕΓΕ
ΑΛΛ' ΕΝ ΟΛΙΓΟΙΣ ΠΟΛΛΑ

Say not little in many words,
but much in few.

ΟΥΔΕΙΣ ΕΛΕΥΘΕΡΟΣ
ΕΑΥΤΟΥ ΜΗ ΚΡΑΤΩΝ

No man is free
who cannot master himself.

*The figure depicts the Pythagorean theorem,
according to which, on a right-angled triangle,
the square of the hypotenuse is equal to the sum
of the squares on the other two sides.*

*The so-called Pythagorean table.
This multiplication table gives the products
of the ten first integers.*

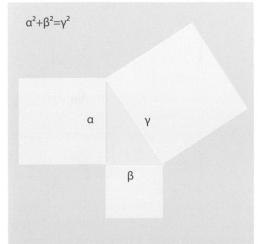

$$\alpha^2 + \beta^2 = \gamma^2$$

1	2	3	4	5	6	7	8	9	10
2	4	6	8	10	12	14	16	18	20
3	6	9	12	15	18	21	24	27	30
4	8	12	16	20	24	28	32	36	40
5	10	15	20	25	30	35	40	45	50
6	12	18	24	30	36	42	48	54	60
7	14	21	28	35	42	49	56	63	70
8	16	24	32	40	48	56	64	72	80
9	18	27	36	45	54	63	72	81	90
10	20	30	40	50	60	70	80	90	100

His life

Mathematician and philosopher who was born on Samos and died in southern Italy, then called Magna Graecia. Pythagoras was the son of a jeweller named Mnesarchus and his beautiful wife Pythais. He is said to have been the first to call himself a philosopher, i.e. lover of knowledge. It happened one day, when Leon, tyrant of Phlious, asked Pythagoras who he was and what he did for a living. He answered: "*I am a philosopher*", thereby coining the word.

Pythagoras was taught by famous philosophers of his age: Pherecydes on Lesbos, Thales and Anaximander in Miletus, and others. On the recommendation of Polycrates, tyrant of Samos, he went to study with Amasis in Egypt where he remained for 22 years. He learned the language of the Egyptians, was initiated into their knowledge, and entered the heart of Egyptian philosophy by studying their books. He went to Babylon, where he stayed for 12 years and became acquainted with Persian magi and wise Chaldeans. Then he travelled to Crete, and, together with Epimenides, he descended into the Idaean Cave on Mt Ida where, according to legend, Rhea had hidden the infant Zeus right after his birth. He also went to Delos and Delphi. Finally he settled in Croton in southern Italy, where he established his own school. This school was something like a political and religious association or brotherhood, and aspired to the social, political and moral reform of the Greek cities, which were then disrupted by partisan political conflicts.

The community of Pythagoreans must have had oligarchic tendencies. The purpose of the society was said to be the creation of wise and virtuous men who would be able to undertake the governance of the cities. In any event, certain mystic rituals were performed in the society, but mathematics, medicine and religion were also taught systematically. The sources report that the society of Pythagoreans consisted of three hundred pupils and followers and that it was not long in acquiring such power that it ruled the state. With such goals in mind, only those men who, after a period of rigorous testing, could show that they were capable of being its loyal and devoted advocates were admitted into the brotherhood. Their origin was not from the masses of the people, but from the noble classes and they were selected, according to the goals of the society, to create a strong and all-powerful organisation which, in conformity with the Egyptian system, would hold the reins of power firmly in its hands. Branches of this school were created by Pythagoras in other towns of southern Italy and Sicily.

In order to achieve the aims of the Pythagorean society, one had to be purged of all weaknesses of the senses and to renounce the customary earthly life. For this reason, the Pythagoreans applied certain ascetic regulations, which appear incomprehensible, but are not, if we consider that the commandments of religions very often represent a rule that exists merely to imbue a group spirit and encourage the members to adopt uniform behaviour. The Pythagorean rules included the following, e.g. not to eat broad beans, not to poke the fire with iron, not to break bread, not to eat the heart, not to touch white cockerels, not to look in the mirror beside the light, not to leave the imprint of their bodies when arising from bed, to stir the ashes when removing the cauldron from the fire so as not to leave its mark.

The teaching of Pythagoras

The most important discovery by Pythagoras was the so-called Pythagorean theorem that contributed to the progress of arithmetic and geometry. According to legend, Pythagoras slaughtered a hundred oxen in order to give thanks to the gods for this discovery. Among Pythagoreans the science of numbers became an object of mystic revelation, in the same way that the first astronomers were astrologers and the first chemists alchemists. In contrast to Thales who was chiefly preoccupied with nature, the Pythagoreans were above all mathematicians who, in the relationships between numbers and in the harmony they express, discovered a kind of matter, which in their opinion, was the principle of the universe.

Pythagoreanism in the subsequent centuries was more or less confused with another occult movement, Orphism, whose founder, an entirely legendary person, was the singer Orpheus from Thrace. His lyre was said to have brought peace to the entire earth, the waves of the sea and wild animals. The Pythagoreans were also musicians. They studied the science of sounds, and measured their intervals in numbers, thus laying the foundations for the acoustic theory of harmony; at the same time they believed in the religious and cleansing power of melody.

Plato was profoundly influenced by both the Pythagorean and Orphic communities. The basic theory taught by Pythagoras and his school was the assurance that the substance of things lies in numbers and in mathematical relations, from which is derived the particular significance of certain numbers: 1 signifies reason and all numbers come from one; 2 is opinion, 3 is wedding, 4 is justice and the square of the first even number, 5 is marriage as the union of the first even with the first odd number (one being separate), 7 expresses health and light, 8 friendship and inventiveness, i.e. the ability of the mind to grasp ideas, 9 is the square of the first odd number.

Of particular importance was 10, the «mystic decade" on which the Pythagoreans swore and which included the first «even-odd", i.e. one, the first even, the first odd and the first square, i.e. 1+2+3+4=10. The opposition of evens and odds lies in the base of a series of other, fundamental oppositions such as the unlimited-limited, rest-motion, male-female, odd-even, one-many, right-left, straight-curved, light-darkness, square-obling, good-evil, etc. This series of oppositions later generates the harmony which is the cha-racteristic of the universe, but which is revealed in particular in musical chords. They even saw the soul as harmony which, within a series of purifications, tended toward the re-velation of the harmony of the spheres.

On the basis of these views, the Pythagoreans built their characteristic cosmology. In particular, they believed that ten heavenly bodies revolve around the central fire. Outside is the heaven of the fixed stars, in the middle is the region of the five planets, the Sun and Moon and blow the sublunar region, the realm of becoming and imperfection. And finally the Pythagoreans hold a significant position in the history of ancient rhetoric. According to them, as medicine heals the body, so music and rhetoric heal the soul. And the art of speech is in essence the elevation and guide of the soul.

ARCHYTAS
OF TARENTUM
430-350 BC

His life and work

Mathematician, engineer, musician, philosopher, governor and politician from Tarentum in southern Italy. We have less information about his life than we have about his activity and teaching. Archytas was an outstanding figure in the public affairs not only if Tarentum, but throughout all of Magna Graecia. He was a friend of Plato's and took an active part in the political life of his homeland. His fellow citizens admired him for his knowledge, high character and personal virtue, and elected him seven times *Strategos, i.e. chief* magistrate of Tarentum, even though the law did not permit one person to hold this office for a period longer than one year. He governed according to the prescriptions of Pythagorean ethics. Regarding the philosophical work of Archytas, we have little information. His scientific work is better known to us. He is regarded as the intellectual leader of Neo-Pythagoreanism. He appears to have regarded the world as a unity consisting of matter and form, and perceived motion as the cause of bodies being formed of matter.

He gave a new form to the old Pythagorean dualism and reshaped it into a dynamic, active world theory. The essence of beings, in his opinion, consisted of a particular unity comprising form and matter. The notion of unity of matter and form appears later as fundamental in Aristotle, who appears to have been significantly influenced by the teaching of Archytas. The primeval motive force (energy) shapes the matter of the elements into bodies. Generally, he viewed motion as the essence of the world. But, as noted above, Archytas worked more as a scientist than as a philosopher.

The study of acoustics and music was considerably advanced by his investigations. For instance, Archytas discovered that the height of a musical tone depends on the frequency of the pulsating movements of the string. He determined arithmetically the relations between tones in the three tonic types: harmonic, chromatic, diatonic. He distinguished between knowledge that has been transmitted and knowledge that stems from discovery by the self-activating individual. He stressed that to ensure the success of any research, the method to be used must first be well known. He invented the rattle to entertain small children and to distract them from the destruction of objects of great value. He applied his conclusions about continuous fractions in the form $a/b=b/c=c/d$ to musical harmony.

View of the Ancient Agora.

PROTAGORAS OF ABDERA

480-410 BC

His life and work

One of the most important Sophists and perhaps the top philosopher of the Sophists school. He was born in Abdera in Thrace which was also the homeland of Democritus. After he started teaching, he did not limit himself to just one city in Greece, but travelled and taught in many. He also spread his activities as far as Sicily and southern Italy, or Magna Graecia, as it was called then.

But the city he preferred and that he visited most often was Athens, where he lived at various periods and developed close relations with all the most important figures of the period such as Euripides, Kallias and Pericles, who in 444 assigned Protagoras to the task of framing laws for Thurii, the newly constituted Athenian colony in Southern Italy. Pericles also entrusted the education and upbringing of his children to Protagoras, showing clearly the extent of his esteem for the teacher. In 410 BC, owing to a book of his entitled *Of the gods*, conservative Athenians convicted him of atheism and disrespect for the gods and his books were symbolically burned in the market. Then Protagoras tried to flee to Sicily, but was drowned on the voyage when his ship sank. Apart from his purely philosophical research, Protagoras was also engaged in rhetoric, grammar, pedagogy and mathematics.

Of his works, *Truth, On conditions at the beginning, On the state, About the Gods*, just a few fragments have been preserved. Some information, however, about his teachings have been saved by various writers such as Plato, who wrote an entire dialogue entitled *Protagoras*.

The core of Protagoras's philosophical teaching can be summarised in the famous phrase we find in the Plato's Theaetetus: «Πάντων χρημάτων μέτρον εστίν άνθρωπος, των μεν όντων ως έστιν, των δε ουκ όντων ως ουκ έστιν" meaning "Man is the measure of all things - of what is, that it is, and of what is not, that it is not."

In terms of the educational aspect of Protagoras's teaching, it should be noted that his main objective was to communicate prudence to his pupils and prepare them to manage their households and take part in civic affairs.

GORGIAS OF LEONTINI
483-376 BC

His life and work

Gorgias was born in Leontini in Sicily and died in Larissa, Thessaly. The most important figure among the ancient Sophists after Protagoras, he was initiated from youth into the philosophy of Empedocles and Eleaticism and into rhetoric, which he learned from the orator Tisias from Syracuse. In 427 BC, he came to Athens at the head of a delegation from his homeland in order to seek military assistance against aggression by Syracuse. The delegation included Tisias. The two emissaries presented themselves in the agora of Athens, where they alternated on the podium arousing the admiration of the crowd. Up to that time, the Athenians had never heard such fascinating orators. And thus they accomplished their mission: Athens allied itself with Leontini. Then Gorgias travelled throughout Greece, and his reputation spread everywhere. He was greatly admired in Boeotia and Thessaly where in Larissa he "succeeded in making the distinguished members of the house of Alevados fall in love with wisdom" and according to tradition, made a great deal of money from practising and teaching rhetoric.

Gorgias wrote a philosophic treatise entitled *On the non-existent* or *On nature*, in which he tried to prove three things: 1) nothing exists; 2) if something does exist, it is unknowable to man and 3) even if something is knowable, knowledge cannot be passed on. With syllogisms that concealed some errors of reason, Gorgias tried to support ontological and epistemological nihilism, i.e., that thought is not identical with being.

In any event rhetoric failed to win over Gorgias. During the Peloponnesian War, Gorgias spoke before Panhellenic gatherings in places like Olympia and Delphi, exhorting the Hellenes to make peace among themselves.

"Τά μέν κατά τῶν βαρβάρων τρόπαια ὕμνους ἀπαιτεῖ,
τα δέ κατά τῶν Ἑλλήνων θρήνους."

meaning

"*Victories against foreigners require festive hymns, against
other Hellenes lamentation.*"

Two rhetorical exercises by Gorgias have been preserved: the *Encomium of Helen* in which he experiments with the nature of discourse and persuasion and *The Defence of Palamedis*, in which he defends a lying and devious man, as well as a small extensive fragment of an Epitaph for the Athenians who were killed in the Peloponnesian War. Gorgias, whose contemporaries praised the magnificence, nobility and grace of his speeches, was the founder of artistic Attic prose, about which it is said that "it must be close to poetry" meaning that it had to be adorned with figures of speech but without exaggeration, that it must by rhythmic but not metered.

The Death of Socrates, *work by David, 18th century.*

SOCRATES

470-399 BC

One of the greatest thinkers and philosophers
of antiquity. He devoted his life and work
to moral philosophy and to the search for moral
good, virtue and justice. The main method he used
was dialectics (the method of seeking
knoweldge by question and answer) by which
he tried to teach men how ignorant they were
and to help them know themselves.
His contribution to philosophy was highly
significant, especially because in Socrates,
it is not the heavenly bodies, earth, clouds etc.
that were of value but the universe
of the human soul.

ΓΝΩΘΙ ΣΑΥΤΟΝ
Know thyself.

ΓΗΡΑΣΚΩ ΑΕΙ ΔΙΔΑΣΚΟΜΕΝΟΣ
I grow old ever learning.

ΟΥΔΕΙΣ ΕΚΩΝ ΚΑΚΟΣ
Nobody is willingly evil.

ΟΥΤΕ ΙΠΠΩ ΧΩΡΙΣ ΧΑΛΙΝΟΥ ΟΥΤΕ ΠΛΟΥΤΩ ΧΩΡΙΣ ΛΟΓΙΣΜΟΥ ΔΥΝΑΤΟΝ ΑΣΦΑΛΩΣ ΧΡΗΣΑΣΘΑΙ
One can safely use neither
a horse without a rein
nor money
without prudence.

ΤΑΣ ΜΕΝ ΠΟΛΕΙΣ ΑΝΑΘΗΜΑΣΙ ΤΑΣ ΔΕ ΨΥΧΑΣ ΜΑΘΗΜΑΣΙ ΔΕΙ ΚΟΣΜΕΙΝ
Cities must be adorned with
statues, souls with virtue.

ΕΝ ΟΙΔΑ, ΟΤΙ ΟΥΔΕΝ ΟΙΔΑ
I know nothing except the fact of my ignorance.

His life

Socrates was born in Athens. He was the son of the sculptor Sophroniscus and the mid-wife Phaenarete. Socrates also practised the trade of sculptor, perhaps up to the age of 40 years old, when he abandoned it and took up philosophy. He soon gathered the young people of the age around him and dedicated his entire life to conversing with and educating them.

It is virtually certain that when he started his dialogues with young people, he neglected his home, as can be concluded from the mocking references by Aristophanes. We know little about his education, so we have to accept that when he was a child, he was educated like other children of the times and that this education was later supplemented by his own efforts. His interests led him to follow the multifaceted cultural events of his age, i.e. performances of ancient tragedy and comedy, and other artistic events, the movement around philosophy, rhetoric, etc. Later he turned to philosophy and eventually acquired the reputation of a wise man. He was married to Xanthippe with whom he had three children. He was spare of diet and satisfied with little. For the upkeep of his family he appeared to have had some small income. It can be regarded as certain that his wealthy friend Criton supported him financially.

Socrates did not involve himself in politics. As a citizen he was disciplined, virtuous and just. He taught obedience to the laws, and provided an example himself, willingly performing his duties as an Athenian citizen. The known events in his life include serving as a hoplite in the expedition of Potidaea during the Peloponnesian War and in the battles of Delium and Amphipolis. During the siege of Potidaea, he saved the life of Alcibiades, as the latter assures us in Plato's *Symposium*, in which he praises the bravery and endurance of Socrates.

Socrates never left Athens again.

Even though Socrates was not a politician, he was nevertheless an extremely well known figure in the city of Athens. His personality was unique, enigmatic and strange. His outer appearance had nothing of Hellenic beauty. He was ugly, with prominent eyes, a bulbous nose with flaring nostrils, thick lips, a bald head and swollen belly. But his soul was that of a splendid man distinguished for his subtlety, intelligence, morality, temperance and self-sufficiency, for the serenity and harmony radiated by his inner world. As Plato said, he was *"excellent, the most prudent and just of the Hellenes"*.

Many people looked upon him with affection, while others, perhaps the majority, disliked him mainly because they saw him as a Sophist. As Alcibiades states in the *Symposium*, externally as a man, Socrates was ugly and looked like a Silene, while on the inside he was beautiful and rich in virtue and wisdom.

His teaching

Socrates dedicated himself to the search for moral philosophy or to the search for the moral good, virtue and justice. He was aware that his main mission in life was to help raise the moral and intellectual level not only of young people, whom he was closest

to and most interested in teaching, but also that of his fellow citizens: to teach people their own ignorance and to help them know themselves («γνῶθι σαυτόν»). The awareness of this mission became deeper within him as he saw the moral order of the Athenian city state being shaken, despite the external brilliance it manifested during the Golden Age of Pericles. He thus tried through his teaching to convince his fellow Athenians that man's primary effort must be the quest for truth and self-control, and that the supreme good lies in the greatest possible cultivation of the soul and in the search for moral prudence. Socrates led to a more human-centred philosophy. This is what Cicero meant when he reported that Socrates took philosophy from the heavens and turned it towards man, towards his soul and his particular nature. In this he influenced all those who came after him. The centre of gravity was no longer the earth, the clouds or the heavenly bodies. What was significant now was the universe that existed within the human soul. Socrates wrote nothing, a fact which has always constituted a problem for historians of philosophy. The only direct sources we have are testimonies by Xenophon, Plato and some comments *from hearsay by Aristotle.* He was not an orator, neither did he teach rhetoric, or give lessons, especially for money, nor travel from one city to another as the Sophists did. He opened no school, but used dialogue. With simple questions, he brought people from all social classes into discussions about religious, ethical, political and social issues. About their lives, the education of their children, justice, virtue etc., i.e. those issues that are generally of interest to man. He would begin the discussion by pretending not to know, but to be interested in learning, e.g. what is justice and injustice, what is courage and cowardice, what is good and bad, beautiful and ugly. The pretence of ignorance used by Socrates in his philosophical discussions is called "Socratic irony".

He never suggested that he was going to teach people something specific, because he believed that if man first learns to use his reason, he will be able to think later, to find and acquire truth by himself. This is why he never offered his interlocutor easy knowledge. It was enough for him to pique his interlocutor with questions, so that the latter could alone arrive to the knowledge he already had within him. This method of Socrates is called "midwifery": just as the midwife draws the child from the belly of its mother, so Socrates drew from his interlocutor whatever the latter had within him, but of which he was of course unaware.

The trial and death of Socrates

As has already been pointed out, there may have been more people who disliked Socrates, because they considered him a Sophist, for what they regarded as his offence against and denial of the institutions of religious and social life. So in 399 BC, three Athenian citizens, Melitus, Anytus and Lycon took him to court on the charge:

«...Ἀδικεῖ Σωκράτης, οὕς μέν ἡ πόλις νομίζει θεούς, οὐ νομίζων, ἕτερα δέ καινά δαιμόνια εἰσφέρων, ἀδικεῖ δέ καί τούς νέους διαφθείρων».

which means:

"Socrates is guilty first of denying the gods recognised by the state in introducing new divinities, and secondly of corrupting the young".

The trial took place in 399 BC. Socrates' pupils had taken care to have a good orator prepared a defence for him, as was the custom then. The famous orator Lysias prepared the defence, in accordance with all the rules of rhetoric. But according to information from Plato's works,

Socrates refused to read it. He said he himself had prepared his defence during his life, through his actions, i.e. always doing what was right. Thus Socrates, with his conscience clear, defended himself as he wished. His own defence, without rhetoric, was certainly not without his usual irony. He told the judges that, in his opinion, no punishment should be imposed on him. On the contrary, it was the obligation of the state, he said, to reward him by maintaining him in the Prytaneum, since he had devoted his life to improving the citizens.

The court judged Socrates guilty and condemned him to death. These charges against Socrates and his death sentence can be understood only within the climate of that age. The climate was then imbued with the disillusionment brought by the defeat of Athens in the Peloponnesian War and the bitter experience of the Thirty Tyrants which followed. The punishment was not carried out immediately, and Socrates remained imprisoned for 30 days.

All during this time, his many pupils flooded the prison, which had been transformed into a true school of philosophy, as Socrates, unruffled and serene, conversed as usual and gave his pupils his last counsels. He rejected the proposals of his pupil Criton, that he escape and save himself, because, up to the last moment of his life, he wanted to be consistent with his teaching and to give a good example of the teaching that "citizens must always respect the laws of the state".

So he drank the cup of hemlock in May of 399 BC, calm and quiet as ever, with resignation and inner peace unique in history, as unique as the personality of the great philosopher and teacher.

Socrates' Voices

The divine voice that Socrates could hear from within
constitutes one of the greatest mysteries
surrounding this great figure of antiquity.
We are accustomed to perceiving this voice as the voice
of God or conscience.

Socrates says:

"Perhaps someone may think it strange that I wander around the city
and do so many things giving advice to each one of you,
but that I do not have the courage to appear publicly and give advice
to the city. The reason for this is something that you have heard me say often,
that I feel inside me something divine and supernatural, something that Melitus
referred to derisively in his charges. And this, which started in my childhood,
is a voice which, when it is heard, urges me not to do something
that I want to do, but it never urges me to do something..."

(Apologia, 31c-32a/I,22)

The Academy of Plato, mosaic floor from Pompeii, 1st century BC. National Museum of Naples.

PLATO

427-347 BC

**One of the most significant thinkers
of antiquity, Plato, despite his aristocratic
origin and his parents' plans for his
political career, devoted his life
to philosophy, first as a devoted pupil
of Socrates, and later by founding
his own school of philosophy, the Academy.
Plato held far-reaching views on the creation
of the world, which have been preserved
in the dialogue Timaeus, while his work
the Republic, is perhaps the world's
most important political science text.**

Ο ΜΗ ΑΔΙΚΩΝ ΟΥΔΕΝΟΣ
ΔΕΙΤΑΙ ΝΟΜΟΥ

He who does no wrong
has no need of the law.

ΕΙ ΑΝΑΓΚΑΙΟΝ ΕΙΗ
ΑΔΙΚΕΙΝ
Η ΑΔΙΚΕΙΣΘΑΙ ΕΛΟΙΜΗΝ
ΑΝ ΑΔΙΚΕΙΣΘΑΙ Η ΑΔΙΚΕΙΝ

If I had either to do wrong
or to be done wrong, I would prefer
to have wrong done to me.

ΔΕΛΕΑΡ ΔΕΙΝΟΝ Η ΗΔΟΝΗ

Pleasure is a terrible temptation.

ΕΑΝ ΜΗ ΟΙ ΒΑΣΙΛΕΙΣ
ΦΙΛΟΣΟΦΗΣΩΣΙΝ
ΟΥΚ ΕΣΤΙ ΔΕΙΝΩΝ ΠΑΥΛΑ

If kings don't reflect,
it is impossible
to be relieved of evil.

Α ΜΗ ΟΙΔΑ
ΟΥΔΕ ΟΙΟΜΑΙ ΕΙΔΕΝΑΙ

If I don't know something,
I don't claim to know it.

Η ΑΓΑΝ ΕΛΕΥΘΕΡΙΑ ΕΟΙΚΕΝ ΟΥΚ ΕΙΣ ΑΛΛΟ
ΤΙ ΕΙΣ ΑΓΑΝ ΔΟΥΛΕΙΑΝ ΜΕΤΑΒΑΜΕΙΝ ΚΑΙ ΙΔΙΩΤΗ ΚΑΙ ΠΟΛΕΙ

Excessive freedom becomes excessive slavery
for both the individual and the state.

His life

Great philosopher and thinker of antiquity. According to tradition, Plato's real name was Aristocles, like his grandfather, and it was only much later that he was called Plato because of the width (*platos*) of his shoulders. He was the son of a distinguished Athenian family said to have been descended from Codros. He was very likely the youngest of his parents' four children. His father's name was Ariston and his mother's Perictione.

He received the education appropriate to the child of a well-to-do and cultivated family, i.e. Homer, Hesiod, music, gymnastics and whatever else an Athenian of the golden age could enjoy. His teachers were Dionysios in reading and writing, Ariston in gymnastics, Dracon in music.

Everybody expected that this extremely gifted young man, who began to write lyric and dramatic poems early in life, would have a brilliant poetic and political career. But things did not work out exactly that way. And when, later, he described a young man of exceptional gifts raised amid nobility and wealth, resisting the enticing exhortations of his relatives and heading toward philosophy, it is obvious that he is reflecting his own personal experiences. Thus, his meeting with Socrates, which occurred when Plato was 20 years old, was of decisive importance. For nine years, he attended lessons in the dialectical method from the wise teacher, who so impressed the young man that throughout history, there has never since been greater devotion on the part of a pupil to a teacher. From then on, his interest in philosophy became the primary concern of his life. In his enthusiasm, in fact, he is said to have burned the poems and tragedies that he had written as a young man and that he was supposedly preparing to present to the public of Athens. In 399 BC, Socrates was sentenced to death and drank hemlock. Plato, disillusioned and perhaps, according to one version, frightened went with other Socratics to Euclid of Megara, an established philosopher They stayed in Megara for about four years after which he returned to Athens, but left again on a number of other voyages.

The first trip was to Egypt, where he learned geometry and astronomy, and to Cyrene in North Africa where he studied with the mathematician Theodore. From there he went to Magna Graecia -the name southern Italy and Sicily was known by at that time- perhaps to become better acquainted with the theories of those Pythagorean communities in which the combination of philosophy and political power was first applied. In this regard Plato believed that cities and men could know happiness and success only when, through divine destiny, either philosophers ruled or kings philosophised.

He tried to take part in political life in Syracuse during the period Dionysius I was tyrant, but he failed and left. The return journey was full of adventures. The ship put him down on Aegina, ally of Sparta, where the Athenian philosopher was regarded as a prisoner of war, because Aegina was then at war with Athens. He was only liberated after a ransom was paid by the wealthy Cyrenaean Anniceris, an old acquaintance of his.

The foundation of the Academy

When he returned to Athens in 387 BC, Plato founded a permanent school of philosophy. The site on which Plato founded his school was a grove called Academus, and thus his school became the Academy. At the Academy astronomy, mathematics and above all philosophy were taught. There, in a beautiful and peaceful natural environment, Plato lived without interruption for twenty years (387-367 BC). He discussed, taught, wrote and published his works. These twenty years were the most fertile and creative years of Plato's life.

Plato's works

The writings of Plato that have come down to us are the *Apologia*, 34 dialogues and the letters, i.e. a total of 36 works. The titles of these 36 works are as follows:

Among the most important of these writings are the: *Symposium, Phaedo, Phaedrus, Republic, Laws, Protagoras, Gorgias, Theaetetus, Parmenides,* and *Timaeus.* Also known are the *Apologia of Socrates* and *Crito.*

Almost all Plato's writings are in the form of a dialogue. Likewise, in virtually all his works, the main person among those discussing in Socrates, who directs the discussion. The vast majority of the dialogues bear the title or name of one of the participants, most often the most important contributor after Socrates. In his dialogues Plato examines all the serious problems of concern to man and develops his philosophical theories, which are thus presented as being Socrates' ideas. It could be said, in other words, that the Platonic dialogue is a representation of Socrates' dialectical method of teaching. The dialogues are written with great literary grace in the language spoken by the Athenians at that period. The philosophic teaching of Plato embraces many issues. He spoke and wrote about the world and its origin, about the soul and knowledge, about mathematics, about the society and the division of labour, about education and art, etc. In his works he makes frequent use of myths to illustrate his ideas and his views of philosophical problems more vividly.

Brief note on Plato's teachings

His philosophy

Plato is an idealist philosopher. He taught that the world around us is not the real world; it is not that which really exists. What really exists, and the reason for the existence of perceived objects are *Ideas.* Ideas are non-material forms inaccessible to our senses; they are immaterial, unchanging, immortal, eternal, and we can sense them only with our minds.Every order of perceived objects corresponds to some Idea from the immaterial world. That is, Plato acknowledges that matter, the perceived world, is a product of some non-material forms, the *Ideas,* which existed prior to matter, beyond and independently of the human mind. The highest of all is the idea of the Good, which is identified with the divinity.

His cosmology

Plato's views of the physical cosmology are contai-ned in the dialogue *Timaeus*, which was written when he was more than seventy years old. There he gives us a mythical narration of the generation of the world, describing how the creator, with the Ideas in mind, created a visible world. Scientific explanations are given regarding the composition of beings, based mainly on mathematical proportions. The genesis of the world was "mixed" since it acquired sub-stance "from the mind and from necessity". Teleological order comes from the mind and mechanical causality comes from the blind resistance of matter.

His political views

Few philosophers have looked with such depth into political phenomena. For Plato, a politician is not so-meone who manages to acquire political power, but only someone who understands what political life is and how it can be built on a solid foundation.

In his *Republic* he gives us a profound analysis of hu-man political life, emphasising that the establishment of a political community is necessary where men cannot avoid it. The task of political philosophy is to study the way in which a perfect republic can be created. And a perfect republic can only be established on the principle of justice. Unjust men cannot establish a perfect republic. The means of making citizens virtuous is education.

TABLE OF PLATO'S WORKS

1. Period of 397-387 BC
The concept of virtue and polemics against the Sophists
a) Socratic dialogues
- *Apologia* (Defence written by Plato for Socrates to defend himself in court).
- *Crito* (loyalty to the laws of the state).
- *Io* (poetry and knowledge).
- *Hippias Minor* (Effort to define the beautiful. Polemic against Sophism).

b) Dialogues on virtue
- *Thrasymachus*, Book 1 Republic (Justice).
- *Laches* (Bravery).
- *Charmides* (Prudence).
- *Euthyphron* (Holiness).
- *Protagoras* (the superiority of philosophy over rhetoric).
- The virtues of the previous four dialogues.

c) Transitional period
- *Gorgias* (In this work, which bears the name of the great Sophist Gorgias, Plato opened the Academy (387 BC). The work is in the nature of a programme, in which criticism is expressed of Athens' political past of Athens and rhetoric is controlled).
- *Menexenus* (polemic against rhetoric)..

2. Period of 386-367 BC.
The great systematic dialogues of his maturity
Main theme: Ideas
- *Euthydemus* (bold ridiculing of the sophisms of the Sophists).
- *Cratylus* (Philosophy of language, against the linguistic theories of the Sophists).
- *Meno* (Teaching of virtue, the theory of memory. First suggestion of the ideas that will constitute the core of Platonic thought).
- *Lysis* (Friendship, love).
- *Symposium* (Philosophical love).
- *Phaedo* (The immortality of the soul).
- *Republic*, books II-X (The ideal republic of reason. This work contains all the themes of Platonic philosophy.)

3. Period of 367-347 BC.
Dialogues of his old age
The great dialectical dialogues
- *Theaetetus* (The theory of knowledge, epistemology)
- *Parmenides* (Ideas and the concepts of dialectics, ontology)
- *Phaedrus* (Philosophical enthusiasm as «mania», the theory of ideas. The three parts of the soul. Psychology and rhetoric.
- *Sophist* (The theory of Being. Ontology. The portrait of the Sophist).
- *Statesman* (Methodology and the theory of the republic).
- *Philebus* (Pleasure. Moral Philosophy and psychology).
- *Timaeus* (Plato's cosmology, physics and biology)
- *Critias* (Philosophy of history. The first period of humanity) Incomplete.
- *Laws* (Plato's final work. He did not have time to publish it. Its theme: providing a model of legislation to assist in the founding of cities.)

XENOCRATES OF CHALCEDON
394-314 BC

His life and teaching

Very few biographical details have come down to us about Xenocrates. We know that he was from Chalcedon, and was the son of Agathenoras. A man with a pure, dig-nified character and with exceptional moral gifts, he was one of Plato's first pupils and suc-ceeded Speusippus as head of Plato's Academy, a position he held until his death. He went to Syracuse together with Plato and Speusippus, where he became acquain-ted with the Pythagoreans of Magna Graecia and their teachings. With Aristotle he made several trips to Asia Minor, where they were engaged in philosophical studies. As a man he was honest and was accustomed to living ascetically. He recommended that people avoid meat and he himself was a vegetarian. Throughout his life he was a model of pure living, which was absolutely in conformity with what he taught. He was abstemious and incorruptible. In fact it is said that the Athenians regarded him as so honest that they per-mitted him to testify in the courts without swearing an oath. He wrote many philosophi-cal works, mostly about ethics.

Diogenes Laertius has left us a list of seventy-five titles, but only fragments of his works have been preserved. He was mainly interested in the nature of the gods and their rela-tions with the heavenly bodies as well as with the practical view of ethics. He under-stood Pythagorean teachings about numbers in depth. He expressed Platonic doctrines intermingled with Pythagorean elements.

It appears that he was the first to distinguish the three main parts of the philosophi-cal system: logic, physics and ethics. Xenocrates admitted three levels of knowledge: thought, sensory perception and opinion. These corresponded to the three forms of be-ing: perceived, understood and composite, about which one can express an opinion. Of these three levels, the perceived is that which exists in the heavens, the understood is that which belongs to all things beyond the heavens, and the level on which one can express an opinion is that which corresponds to the heavens, because this is visible with the senses and comprehensible through astronomy. The intention of Xenocrates was to elaborate Plato's theories systematically. A significant position in his thought was held by mathematical metaphysics, which continued the Platonic theory of ideas-numbers. Thus he believes that all reality results from the interaction of two oppo-sing principles: the One and «the indeterminate dyad". The dyad is responsible for multip-licity or diversity, evil and motion, whereas the One is responsible for unity, good and rest.

ΠΑΝΤΕΣ ΓΑΡ ΓΑΙΗΣ ΤΕ ΚΑΙ ΥΔΑΤΟΣ ΕΓΕΝΟΜΕΘΑ
We are all of earth and water made.

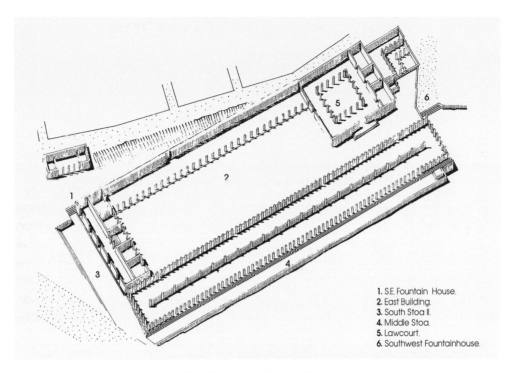

1. S.E. Fountain House.
2. East Building.
3. South Stoa II.
4. Middle Stoa.
5. Lawcourt.
6. Southwest Fountainhouse.

Plan of the Ancient Agora of Athens.

The Stoa of Attalos houses the museum of the Ancient Agora of Athens.

ARISTOTLE

384-322 BC

Aristotle was the greatest systematic
philosopher of antiquity. He was the first
to philosophise on the basis of science.
Because of his great knowledge, especially
in the physical sciences, he became known
in history as a "panepistimon" or man of all
sciences. Aristotle developed the dialectical
method in logic, not in the Socratic sense
of the dialogue but as a process consisting
of thesis, antithesis and synthesis,
which then becomes the new thesis.

ΠΑΝΤΕΣ ΑΝΘΡΩΠΟΙ ΦΥΣΕΙ ΤΟΥ ΕΙΔΕΝΑΙ ΟΡΕΓΟΝΤΑΙ

All men possess by nature
the desire to know.

ΕΞΙΣ ΔΕΥΤΕΡΑ ΦΥΣΙΣ

Habit becomes
second nature.

ΟΠΟΥ ΑΜΙΛΛΑ ΚΑΙ ΝΙΚΗ ΕΣΤΙ

Wherever there is a contest,
there is also victory.

Ω ΦΙΛΟΙ, ΦΙΛΟΣ ΟΥΔΕΙΣ

Oh friends,
no friend exists.

ΑΝΘΡΩΠΟΣ ΖΩΟΝ (ΦΥΣΕΙ) ΠΟΛΙΤΙΚΟΝ

Man is by nature
a political animal.

ΜΙΑ ΧΕΛΙΔΩΝ ΕΑΡ ΟΥ ΠΟΙΕΙ

One swallow doesn't make a spring.

His life

Aristotle was born in Stagira, Macedonia and died in Chalcis. His father Nicomachus was court physician to Amyntas II king of Macedonia. His mother's name was Phaestias.

He came to Athens at the age of 18 and became a pupil of Plato's at his famous Academy, where he studied for 20 years, i.e. until his great teacher died. During this period he made profound studies of Platonic philosophy, mathematics, physics, astronomy, rhetoric, political sciences, logic, etc. Later he devoted himself to each one of these subjects separately, and differently from the way in which they had preoccupied Plato, i.e. more realistically. In the meantime, he laid the foundations for his own philosophy. After Plato's death, he established a school of rhetoric in Athens. In 342 BC, he was invited by King Philip of Macedonia to undertake the education of his son Alexander, then thirteen years old. The philosopher exerted a great influence on the spirit and soul of Alexander, and the latter was always grateful to his great teacher.

In 335, Aristotle returned to Athens where his founded his own School in the Lyceum and called it Peripatetic. The origin and significance of this name has not to this day been satisfactorily explained. Aristotle worked for thirteen years as head of the School and writer of philosophical works. He held a significant post in Athens until the moment Alexander died, in June of 323 BC. After Alexander's death, the Athenians immediately began trying to liberate themselves from the domination of the Macedonians. They knew that Aristotle had come from Macedonia and that he had personal relations with Philip, Alexander and the powerful general Antipater. A trial was held. In order to avoid conviction and its consequences, Aristotle fled during the trial to Chalcis in Euboea, where his mother's family had a house and where a Macedonian guard looked after his personal safety.

Contrary to Plato, it appears that he was in ill health for most of his life. He became ill in Chalcis and died in the summer of 322 AD.

TABLE OF WORKS BY ARISTOTLE

1. **Logic: Tool:** a) Categories b) On Interpretation c) Prior Analytics (2 books) d) Posterior Analytics (2 books), e) Topics (8 books), f) Sophistical Refutations.
2. **Physics:** a) Physics (8 books), b) On the Heavens (4 books), c) On Generation and Corruption (3 books), d) Meteorology (4 books).
3. **Biology:** a) History of Animals (10 books), b) Parts of Animals (4 books), c) Progression of Animals, d) Movement of Animals, e) Generation of Animals (5 books).
4. **Psychology:** On the Soul (3 books), including a group entitled Parva Naturalia, to which belong the following: a) On the Senses and their Objects, b) On Memory and Recollection, c) On Sleep and Waking, d) On Dreams, e) On Length and Shortness of Life, f) On Life and Death, g) On Respiration.
5. **Metaphysics:** Metaphysics (12 books).
6. **Ethics:** a) Eudemian Ethics (7 books), b) Magna moralia, c) Nicomachean Ethics (10 books).
7. **Politics:** a) Politics (8 books), b) Constitution of Athens, c) Economics (2 books).
8. **Aesthetics and Literature:** a) Rhetoric (3 books), b) Poetics.
9. **Problems**

His work

Aristotle was a prolific writer. he wrote a total of four hundred works, an encyclopedia of philosophical and scientific knowledge, about anything learnable. Of them about forty complete works have been preserved and fragments of another hundred or so. Unfortunately for the history of literature, whatever has been preserved of his writings are lectures intended for his pupils, and were not written for the broader public. His works were addressed to the non-initiated, in order to lead them progressively toward strict science; in other words, the works that would have been of greatest interest to us have been lost. Those that have been preserved are of a technical nature with only moderate literary value. Language was just a means of communication with someone else and not, as was usually the case with Plato, music or poetic magic.

Of Aristotle's large output, 143 titles of his works have come down to us, divided into the categories listed in the table below.

Books of logic: The first work *Categories* deals with the main forms of statements regarding substance (*ousia*) or being (*on*). *On Interpretation* is a treatise on judgement. *Prior Analytics* talks about syllogistic thought. *Posterior Analytics* talks about proof, definition and division, as well as about knowledge of principles. *Topics* is concerned with dialectical syllogisms. And finally, *Sophistical Refutations* discusses the fallacious reasoning used by the Sophists when they want to refute a premise, and endeavours to disprove the seeming validity of their arguments.

Metaphysics: In his work *Metaphysics*, Aristotle criticises Plato's theory of ideas and offers a solu-tion to the ontological problem regarding the explanation of being, where Aristotle acknowledges four causes, the material and formal causes, and the final and efficient causes.

Writings about natural things, zoology and the physical sciences: One of Aristotle's most useful services to humanity was his theory of biological order which is based on observation around the purposeful structure of living organisms. Aristotle saw examples of the order of Nature in events like: the living creatures that grow out of sperm, the instinct to act in a certain way that is shown in its varied manifestations in animals, the ability of the organs to adapt.

Ethical and political writings: Aristotle places above all the intellectual energy of the mind; its thoughtful virtues, in his opinion, contain their own special delight. This ideal is expressed in the characteristic distinction between physical labour, which was the fate of slaves, and intellectual work, the prerogative of free citizens. Aristotle's ethical ideal was God, the "embodiment of wisdom". In his political writings, Aristotle distinguishes three good and three evil forms of governance of a state. He regards as good those forms within which the possibility of reaping profit from the use of power was precluded, whereas power itself should be used to serve the society as a whole. These forms are: the kingdom, the aristo-cracy and the "republic" (power of the middle class), based on a combination of oligarchy and democracy. On the other hand, he regarded tyranny, pure oligarchy, and extreme democracy as evil, corrupted variations of these forms.

Aesthetics and literature: His *Poetics*, a teacher's notebook, half-finished and his *Rhetoric*, in three books, are valuable works, necessary for anyone who wants to study the literary history of Greece. Both books are full of new, astute views, because Aristotle had thought as much and as deeply about the works of the poets and orators as he had about natural history, physics and metaphysics. Aristotle regarded art as a particular type of knowledge and ranks it higher than knowledge of history. In his works on aesthetics and literature, he formu-lated a theory about artistic creation and provided theoretical explanations of epic poetry and tragedy.

The Lyceum and the Peripatetics

The term Lyceum comes from the Lyceum grove in the northeastern part of ancient Athens, where there was a sanctuary to Lyceus Apollo. This was where the Peripatetic school of philosophy founded by Aristotle in 335 BC was based. It was one of the best *gymnasia* in ancient Athens, near Ardettos and Palladio.

The Lyceum grove was initially the site for practising cavalry manoeuvres. It was surrounded by high trees, most of which were plane trees, and covered with grass and other vegetation. Nearby were the sources of the Eridanos River and the fountain of Panopos.

It extended from present day Syntagma Square towards the National Garden, where traces can be found of the foundation of a temple that was probably dedicated to Lyceus Apollo. The natural beauty of the site quickly drew philosophers there, who transformed it into an intellectual gymnasium. In antiquity, these schools were places where all types of intellectual activity were cultivated. That was where philosophers discussed philosophical problems, and where Aristotle established his *Peripatetic School* in which he taught for 13 years. It was likewise a place frequented by Socrates and where the famous Sophist Protagoras taught. Scholars frequently identify the Lyceum with Aristotle's Peripatos or Peripatetic School, but they were not the same thing. The *Lyceum* is a location, while the Peripatos expresses more an activity that took part on that site. The area of the Lyceum was called "peripatos" because of the fact that philosophical classes were held there, during which the teacher and pupils were not seated but walked around (=*peripatos*). Again, disciples of this particular school of philosophy were called «Peripatetics", which also expressed a specific philosophical trend.

Generally, the Peripatetic school remained loyal to the basic principles of Aristotelian teaching. Some of its representatives added new ideas or supplemented Aristotelianism with more detailed explanations.

After the death of Aristotle, various philosophical currents held sway in his Lyceum. The school was initially oriented in a naturalist direction and characterised by breadth of learning (Theophrastus, Eudemus of Rhodes, Aristoxenus of Tarentum, Dicaearchus, Clearchus, Demetrius of Phaleron). Thus Theophrastus, the first of Aristotle's successors, and Eudemus followed their own path toward Logic, while Aristoxenus introduced Pythagorean elements into its ethical precepts. During the early Hellenistic years, the empiricist tendency was reinforced (Straton of Lampsacus) while those who continued in the direction of broad learning included Hermippus, Sotion, Satyrus, Heracleides of Lembus, Agatharchides and Demetrius of Byzantium. Attempts were made by Hieronymus of Rhodes, Critolaus, Diodorus of Tyre and others to establish contact with other schools of philosophy. Later, the Peripatetics turned once again to the works of Aristotle.

After them, peripatetic thought was no longer renewed and turned its attention solely to the documented research of the Aristotelian tradition. Before the end of the 3rd century AD, philosophic studies were monopolised by the School of the Neoplatonists.

PLOTINUS

205-270 AD

**He was the most important
Neoplatonic philosopher
and an outstanding intellectual
in the period of waning antiquity.
Plotinus taught the inner, spiritual
life and urged people to turn
to their inner world.**

ΟΥΔΕ ΤΟ ΚΑΛΟΝ ΑΝ
ΙΔΟΙ ΨΥΧΗ ΜΗ ΚΑΛΗ
ΓΕΝΟΜΕΝΗ. ΓΕΝΕΣΘΩ
ΔΕ ΠΡΩΤΟΝ ΘΕΟΕΙΔΗΣ,
ΠΑΣ ΚΑΙ ΚΑΛΟΣ ΠΑΣ,
ΕΙ ΜΕΛΕΙ ΘΕΑΣΑΣΘΑΙ
ΘΕΟΝ ΤΕ ΚΑΙ ΚΑΛΟΝ

A soul cannot see beauty
if it is not beautiful itself.
So let every man first become
divine and beautiful if he wants
to see god and this beauty.

Plotinus writes:
"Let us turn totally inward", he writes. "God is not outside any being. He is within all beings,
but they do not know it. They become remote from Him or rather remote from
their own selves. The wise man is turned toward himself and finds all things therein".

"I frequently wake up having left my body; detached from everything I see
the most exquisite beauty that one can imagine. At such moments I am convinced
that I possess a higher destiny. I am one with the divine being and I am reflected
within him, above all unthinking beings..."

His life and work

Plotinus was born in Lycopolis in Egypt and died in Rome. He was the most important representative of Neoplatonism and the most significant intellectual in the period of declining antiquity. He accompanied Emperor Gordian III on his campaign against the Persians, and in the process became acquainted with Persian and Indian philosophy. After the fall of Gordian, Plotinus fled to Antioch and from there to Rome. In Rome he set up his school in 244 AD at which, for 26 continuous years, he lectured in front of large and heterogeneous audiences.

In Rome he was generally esteemed for his moderation, his noble convictions and the purity of his ethics; the Emperor Gallienus and his wife Salonina were among his enthusiastic admirers.

Plotinus lived his personal life absolutely in accordance with his philosophical principles, i.e. in an ascetic way: he slept little, ate little, avoided meat, remained celibate, and would not allow himself to sit for a painter to make an image of an "image". He likewise praised a praetor friend of his for resigning from his position, giving away his property, liberating his slaves and, fasting every other day, trying to achieve the ideal of being satisfied with little. Plotinus began writing at the age of fifty. His writings were published by Porphyry* after his death, arranged in groups of nine treatises in each group. For this reason they were called the *Enneads* (*ennea*–nine).

Subject of the Enneads

1st Ennead: The Individual, **2nd & 3rd Enneads:** The world of the senses,

4th Ennead: The Soul, **5th Ennead:** The Nous (Mind-Spirit),

6th Ennead: Being and Oneness

His teaching in essence demonstrates his profound knowledge of all ancient Greek philosophy, and contains elements of mysticism that sometimes constituted a new element in his philosophy. He believed in one god, the divine One, from which the world was created through emissions of force.

The primeval being (*the First*) has no limit, form or determination; it is unlimited and unending. It has no attributes; it is without magnitude, without life, without thought. The One is that which is beyond and above all being and intellect. Plotinus was a teacher of the interior and spiritual life. The words «πάντα εσω» (*always within*) could be used as an emblem of his system. According to him, there are three «persons" that make up the human mind: the One, the Nous (mind - spirit) and the Soul; and only three categories of beings can be elevated: musicians, lovers and philosophers. Plotinus was the last of the great philosophers of antiquity.

Plotinus writes: "The Fates and their mother, Necessity, rotate the spindle and weave the fate of each person at the moment of birth". (ancient greek: «Αἱ Μοῖραι δέ καί ἡ Ἀνάγκη μήτηρ· οὖσα στρέφουσι καί ἐν τῇ γενέσει ἑκάστου ἐπικλώθουσι».

---

*Porphyry: Neoplatonist philosopher from Tyre, pupil and successor of Plotinus, 233-304 AD.

CHRYSIPPUS OF CILICIA

281-205 BC

His life and work

Philosopher from Tarsus (or Soli) in Cilicia in the 3rd century BC. He is regarded as the reinvigorator of Stoic philosophy and the expressor of Stoic orthodoxy. He was educated in Athens where he attended the classes of Cleanthes, and perhaps of Zeno, but also under Arcesilaus and Lacydes, heads of the Middle Academy. Every day he wrote about 500 lines, that eventually amounted to a total of 705 works. Some 311 of these were writings of dialectical and logical content. Just a few fragments have been saved. Perhaps because of the large volume of his writings, the style of his treatises was unpolished and dry, although his arguments were said to have been lucid. Chrysippus took on the task of assimilating, developing and systematising the doctrines that came down to him. It was he who gave final form to Stoicism, and about him it was said "Had it not been for Chryssipus, there would be no Stoa*. But it was Chrysippus alone, the third great leader of the Stoics, who managed to guide the school onto a scientific path. In ac-cordance with the general principle of Stoicism, for Chrysippus, there was only the physical world, which is perceived by our senses through the infinite complexity and diversity of various other bodies. Chrysippus battled furiously against the concept of chance and taught that the apparent lack of cause for particular events was due to some causality inaccessible to human knowledge. The single spirit of the universe, whose seat the Stoics placed sometimes in the heavens, sometimes in the sun and at other times in the centre of the world, inheres in all things as the force that gives them life. Diseases are the necessary concomitant of the natural laws that do not depart from their objective. In fact, they have the special moral significance of serving divine providence, either as morally improving punishment or as an opportunity to exercise moral powers. The universe is one. It is ruled by Reason that springs from the divine and governs all nature. The necessity that dominates it and expresses a specific structure is fate and providence together.

---

*Stoa: long, narrow building usually open on one or two sides, either part of another building or an independent structure whose roof rests on rows of columns. In ancient Greece, people would gather in stoes and discuss. The philosopher Zeno taught in the Poikile Stoa (Painted Colonnade) and for this reason his philosophy was called Stoa or Stoic philosophy.

POSEIDONIUS
OF APAMEA OR RHODES
135 BC-50 BC

His life and work

Stoic philosopher from Apamea in Syria. A man of restless and inquiring mind, Poseidonius, whose interests embraced many subjects, travelled in Egypt, Africa, Gaul, Liguria and Sicily. Finally, in 97 BC, he moved to Rhodes where he became head of the Stoic School. In Rhodes he engaged in politics as well, and was made Governor of the Rhodian city-state. His long years of residence in Rhodes was the reason for his being called Rhodian. In fact Rhodes sent him as its ambassador to Rome in 86 BC.

He had personal relations with famous Romans who honoured him, including Pompey and Cicero. The latter, apart from admiring his great learning, was also his pupil in Rhodes in 78 BC. Pompey visited his school twice to pay homage to the great sage.

Poseidonius wrote extensively, although his works are now lost. To his credit are more than 24 works from which one can conclude the breadth of his interests: *On the ocean and what is in it, On meteors, On the magnitude of the sun, Natural reason, On the gods, On destiny, On prophesy, On heroes and demons, On emptiness, On the world, Explanations of Plato's Timaeus, On virtues, On passions, On duty, Preventive reasons, Histories.* In the last book which is also called *History after Polybius,* he covered events from 145-85 BC; it filled 52 books.

The philosophical views of Poseidonius are characterised by his intention of reconciling all the useful truths of previous philosophy into a large harmonious whole. Thus he can be described as both a Stoic and a Heraclitan, a pre-Socratic and a Platonist. He developed the mystical trends of Stoicism and Platonism to a large degree and thus opened the way for Neoplatonism in the 3rd century AD.

His world theory is founded on the total empirical knowledge of his time and soothes the human soul. He insists on a middle position for man, earthly in body and super-earthly in his soul and, therefore, capable of growth in both spheres of the universe. The contribution of Poseidonius to the investigation of nature was particularly significant:
- He confirmed the relationship between the tides and the phases of the Moon.
- He tried to calculate the magnitude of the sun and its distance from earth
- He calculated the circumference of the earth, made a globe and drew a world map.

DIOGENES OF SINOPE

410-323 BC

The head of the Cynic School of philosophy, Diogenes's «provocative» way of life and his brilliant rejoinders were in absolute harmony with his philosophical principles. Diogenes recommended that one abstain from acquiring material goods and limit one's self to the absolutely necessary.

ΤΟ ΕΝ ΤΗ ΚΑΡΔΙΑ
ΤΟΥ ΝΗΦΟΝΤΟΣ
ΕΠΙ ΤΗΣ ΓΛΩΣΣΗΣ
ΤΟΥ ΜΕΘΥΟΝΤΟΣ

What a sober man keeps in his heart is what the drunken man reveals in his words.

ΠΕΝΙΑ ΑΥΤΟΔΙΔΑΚΤΟΣ
ΑΡΕΤΗ

Poverty is a self-taught virtue.

ΑΝΘΡΩΠΟΝ ΖΗΤΩ

I'm looking for a man.

His life and work

Diogenes of Sinope, son of Icesias, was the leader of the Cynic philosophers. He spent many years of his life in Athens and died in Corinth. Tradition reports that his father, a money-changer, was convicted of adulterating the coinage and that Diogenes was included in the charge.

Tradition tells us that asked his father:

"Why can't we make our own money?"

Whether or not he was a pupil of Antisthenes has not been absolutely confirmed, the fact remains that he was clearly influenced by his teaching. Utilising the ascetic morals of Antisthenes, Diogenes went even further, supporting as basic principles absolute self-sufficiency and that man should limit himself to covering only needs that were absolutely necessary to his survival. His life was a model of the principles he preached, characteristic of which was the fact that he always wore cheap fabrics, and never cut his beard, expressing in this way his indifference to material goods. He always had a sack on his shoulder in which he carried all his belongings. Also, he lived inside a terracotta jar.

Some sources report that Diogenes was captured by pirates on a voyage, sold as a slave to a Corinthian named Xeniades, and lived in Corinth for the rest of his life, preaching the doctrines of virtuous self-control.

His provocative behaviour, his blasphemy and his characteristic wit often be-came, according to tradition, an occasion for creating a rich store of anecdotes.

One characteristic example is the famous meeting between Alexander the Great and Diogenes in 336 BC. At that time Diogenes was in Corinth and Alexander called all those distinguished Greeks who recognised him as leader of the Hellenes to come to Isthmus and take part in the campaign against the Persians that he was planning. Diogenes did not show up. Then Alexander went to meet him. He found the philosopher next to his jar, and approaching, asked the latter if he desired any favour whereupon Diogenes, who was at that moment sitting in the sun, replied with the apathy typical of him:

"I want you to get out of my light".

He was called Cyon (Dog) because of his apathy. The Cynics tried in some way to imitate the dogs' way of life: they were not interested in acquiring culture and did not care about other peoples' opinions of their way of life. By extension anything that resembled the Cynics' brash honesty was called cynicism.

Regarding his work, it is disputed. Diogenes' way of life was anything but conducive to writing activities. But many of his witty remarks have been saved. His philosophical principles had great impact in the Hellenistic and Roman periods. The emperor Julian in fact was a fanatic supporter of Cynic philosophy.

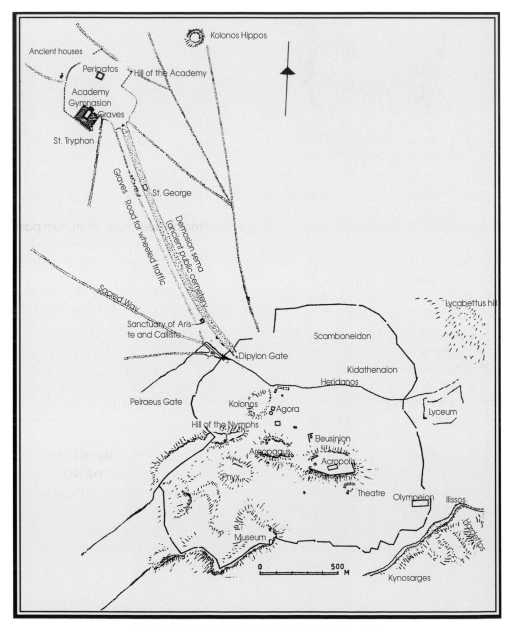

Topography of ancient Athens (Travlos 1971, Wycherley 1978).

EPICURUS
OF SAMOS

341-270 BC

ΟΥΔΕΝ ΙΚΑΝΟΝ Ω
ΟΛΙΓΟΝ ΤΟ ΙΚΑΝΟΝ

Nothing is enough for him
who regards the sufficient as little.

ΤΟΥΣ ΑΦΡΟΝΑΣ
Ο ΧΡΟΝΟΣ ΤΟΥΣ
ΔΕ ΦΡΟΝΙΜΟΥΣ Ο ΛΟΓΟΣ
ΤΗΣ ΛΥΠΗΣ ΑΠΑΛΛΑΤΤΕΙ

Time delivers foolish men from pain,
and reason intelligent men.

With his view that nature determines
natural phenomena rather than the gods,
He freed man from the fear of a punishing god.
The supreme good, according to Epicurus is
pleasure, because all living creatures
seek pleasure and avoid pain.
His maxim about death is particularly well
known, i.e. that it does not concern us
because as long as we exist, death does not
and when he exists we do not.

Ο ΔΙΚΑΙΟΣ
ΑΤΑΡΑΚΤΟΤΑΤΟΣ,
Ο Δ'ΑΔΙΚΟΣ
ΤΑΡΑΧΗΣ ΓΕΜΩΝ

The just man always has peace
in his soul, while the unjust man
is full of great tumult.

ΛΑΘΕ ΒΙΩΣΑΣ

Live in obscurity.

ΓΕΛΑΝ ΑΜΑ ΔΕΙΝ ΚΑΙ ΦΙΛΟΣΟΦΕΙΝ

One must be able to philosophise and laugh at the same time.

His life

A personality with great moral persuasion, he attached great significance to the friendship that linked him with his pupils. Having previously studied the teachings of many philosophers, he started teaching in Mytilene in 311 BC and then established a school at Lampsacus, to which he attracted several disciples. We are told that the inhabitants of Lampsacus so admired his ideas and character that they collected the amount of 80 *minae* and bought him a house with a garden in Athens, the famous *Garden of Epicurus* where he was the venerated head of a remarkable, and up to that time unique, society of men and women, among whom were free citizens as well as slaves, serfs, housewives and courtesans. The courtesan Leontia was his mistress and his pupil. Epicurus lived with Stoic simplicity and was extremely spare of diet. All those who knew him described him as a considerate, self-sufficient and virtuous man and thus the linking of his name with a life of pleasure is in full opposition to the truth.

His work

Epicurus was a voluminous writer, comparable only to Chrysippus. According to Diogenes Laertius, his work was contained in about 300 rolls. But unfortunately, only a fraction of this enormous oeuvre, has been preserved:
a) three didactic letters to Herodotus, Pythocleas and Meniceas, the first and third of which contain a brief summary of nature and ethics; the second discusses meteorology, although its authenticity has been questioned.
b) 37 books (incomplete) of his work *On Nature* which were preserved in the charred traces of the rolls discovered at Herculaneum.
c) the *Canon* in one book, which sets out Epicurus's theory of knowledge and
d) many maxims, 80 of which were found in the Vatican Library in 1888.

His teaching, as is the case with many philosophical writings of antiquity, consists of three branches: logic, physics and ethics. Epicurus denied any teleological interpretation and any kind of Providence to explain natural phenomena. The gods exist in blessedness in a transcendent world and do not interfere in the movements of nature and human life. Physics is what helps us to understand natural causes. This knowledge frees man from fear of the gods and of death.

Religion, according to Epicurus, goes hand in hand with and flourishes under ignorance and casts the shadow of fear of heavenly spies, i.e. the gods, over life. Regarding ethical problems, three of his writings are mentioned, the most significant of their kind: *On the end, On heretics and those who are to be avoided, On lives.* Epicurean ethics had a materialist basis. It was based on the view that the supreme good is pleasure. Of course, there are pleasures that result in pain, sometimes very great. But the wise man avoids such deceptive pleasures. Epicurus admitted that there were physical pleasures, such as food, sleep etc. which can offer some happiness, but that this was ephemeral. The wise man can of course limit these to what is absolutely necessary: with a little bread and water he can be as happy as Zeus. On the contrary, intellectual pleasures are not limited to the present but extend into the past, as memories and into the future, as hopes. Epicurus taught that the ideal was to live unnoticed, outside of social turmoil, in the context of a philosophical companionship and friendship, winning harmonious existence and *calm*.

According to the Epicurean philosopher Philodemus, the entire teaching of the Epicurean school can be summarised in a few words:

«Ἄφοβον ὁ θεός, ανύποπτον ὁ θάνατος,
τό ἀγαθόν εὔκτητον, το δεινόν εὐκαρτέρητον».

meaning

"Unfearing of God, unsuspecting of death,
the good easily obtained, suffering to be borne patiently".

The spirit of Epicurus exerted a major influence in his own time and even during the early Christian period. But his views of distant gods and absolute calm were interpreted by many Christian writers as manifesting atheism, a fact which caused the dissolution of his school in the 4th century AD. During more recent years, the scholarly approach to Epicurus' writings has attributed to his work the merit it justly deserves in philosophical thought up to the present day.

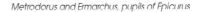

Metrodorus and Ermarchus, pupils of Epicurus

ARTISTS
...THE CELEBRATION OF BEAUTY

The second chapter is devoted to all those whose works praised life and beauty. First of all were the poets:

▸ Homer and Hesiod, the main representatives of epic poetry whose themes were mainly taken from the great wars, the misfortunes and triumphs of a people.

▸ Sappho, Archilochus, Alcaeus, Alcman, Pindar and Bacchylides, as representatives of lyric poetry that was always recited to the accompaniment of music in general or the lyre in particular.

▸ Theocritus, as a representative of the poetic genre of the idyll, which prospered during the Hellenistic period, on themes from rural and especially pastoral life, and was of a tender, and erotic nature.

▸ The Alexandrian Callimachus Callimachus, who lived between 323 and 240 BC.

▸ Then there were the great tragedians Aeschylus, Sophocles and Euripides.

Tragedy is a form of solemn drama in which the hero suffers and often dies in such a way as to lead the spectator to psychological "catharsis". As a genre, it was born of the religious songs sung by the chorus at the feasts of Dionysus. The dancers, representing the followers of the god, appear as Satyrs who looked like goats *(tragoi)* from which the word *tragedy* is derived (i.e. goat-song). Tragedy developed from song into drama with the introduction of actors. According to tradition, it was Thespis in 554 BC who interrupted the choral odes with the speech of an actor (sometimes it was a narrative monologue and at others there was a dialogue with the Coryphaeus of the chorus). Later the three great tragedians Aeschylus, Sophocles and Euripides shaped tragedy as a genre and introduced various innovations.

The representatives of ancient comedy were Aristophanes and the younger Menander. Comedy is a theatrical work that creates mirth by satirising characters, social manners, and political life. Ancient comedy emerged from the Dionysiac feasts and in particular from the vulgar remarks one celebrant would address to another. It developed mainly in Athens. The comedy of the ancient Greeks can be divided into *ancient comedy*, which satirised people and political events, *later comedy*, which satirised manners, and *intermediate comedy*, which constituted the transitional stage between ancient and later comedy.

The poets are followed by the presentation of the most important sculptors of ancient Greece (Phidias, Polyclitus, Paeonius, Praxiteles, Lyssipus, Scopas) who created monumental works and became landmarks in the world history of art.

And finally, Polygnotus and Zeuxis are presented from the pantheon of ancient Greek painting.

"The Three Muses", bas-relief plaque from the base of the constitution of the Apollonian Triad, a work by Praxiteles, 330-320 BC. Athens. National Archaeological Museum.

I. POETRY
A. EPIC POETRY

Odysseus in the Cyclops' cave. (Homer's Odyssey).
Early Attic copy, c. 670 BC, Archaeological Museum of Eleusina.

HOMER

Mid 9th - early 8th cent. BC

The greatest of the epic poets.
The two great epic masterpieces,
the Iliad and the Odyssey,
are attributed to him.
The precise date and place of his
birth have not been established.
Tradition holds the poet
to have been blind.

ΕΙΣ ΟΙΩΝΟΣ ΑΡΙΣΤΟΣ
ΑΜΥΝΕΣΘΑΙ ΠΕΡΙ
ΠΑΤΡΗΣ

Fight for your country
that is the best, the only omen.

ΑΕΙΝ ΑΡΙΣΤΕΥΕΙΝ
ΚΑΙ ΥΠΕΙΡΟΧΟΝ
ΕΜΜΕΝΑΙ ΑΛΛΩΝ

Always to be best, and to be
distinguished above the rest.

ΟΥΔΕΝ ΓΛΥΚΙΟΝ
ΠΑΤΡΙΔΟΣ

Nothing is sweeter than home.

ΟΙΚΩΦΕΛΙΗ, Η ΤΕ ΤΡΕΦΕΙ
ΑΓΛΑΑ ΤΕΚΝΑ

Orderliness produces
bright children.

ΑΝΙΗ ΚΑΙ ΠΟΛΥΣ ΥΠΝΟΣ

Too much sleep can be distressing.

His life

Homer is the greatest poet who ever lived. After a great deal of controversy, literary disputations and research, as well as the examination of evidence derived from various sources, there no longer seems to be any doubt about the actual existence of the poet Homer. Born either on the Aegean island of Chios or in the city of Smyrna in Asia Minor, he composed at least two poems, the *Iliad* and the *Odyssey*, works acknowledged worldwide as masterpieces. He is portrayed as blind; this is due to the assumption that he was the blind poet referred to in a hymn to Apollo. Such an interpretation is, however, unsubstantiated.

His work

Literary scholarship has attributed to Homer a body of poetic invention, which cannot be conclusively assigned to him. But as the subject of the unity in the composition of the two epic poems -the *Iliad* and the *Odyssey*- became the subject of so much controversy, there ensued an entire *Homeric Question* centering on this matter that remains to this day largely unresolved. It is however indisputable that the two great Homeric works, the *Iliad* and the *Odyssey*, have for three thousand years have provided humanity with cultural sustenance, as well as models of unparalleled art that raise their creator to the position of eternal mentor and master of all types of literary art, be it poetry, theater, narrative, or rhetoric. Homer had already reached the peak of his fame during the 7th century BC; while from the 6th century BC on, his entire work was recited every four years during the Panathenian Games. After the fifth century BC his work was studied in schools and his aphorisms were known throughout most of Greece. Plato remarked that it was to Homer that Greece owed its learning.

The Iliad: The poem is steeped in the spirit of war. In its pages, praise is reserved mostly for military skill. As the towering figure of the *Iliad* is Achilles, one might expect the epic to be titled the *Achilliad* instead. Its title *Iliad* came from *Ilion* (i.e. Troy) the city where the events narrated took place. In the 12th century BC Greek tribes conquered and burned the then powerful city of Troy that stood on the Asian coast of the Hellespont. Popular imagination turned this historic event into the legends of the Trojan War. The tale of the *Iliad* centers on Achilles' rage against Agamemnon and its terrible consequences. The entire action takes place within fifty-two days, four of which are the most dramatic and crucial to the outcome. The *Iliad* is a dense epic poem of 15,537 verses, divided into twenty-four books.

The Odyssey: In the *Odyssey* Homer used his outstanding poetic imagination to create from the tale of Odysseus' return to this homeland a work in which mythical elements abound. Yet, in contrast to the warlike character of the *Iliad*, the atmosphere of the entire poem is calm and peaceful. The *Odyssey* is shorter than the *Iliad*, consisting as it does of 12,080 verses; it too, however, is divided into twenty-four books.

THE ILIAD

Book One: Apollo has sent a plague to strike the camp of the Achaeans (i.e., the Greeks) in order to avenge the old priest Chryses whose pleas for the return of his daughter, given to Agamemnon as a war prize by the Achaeans, were rejected offensively. After much deliberation, Agamemnon is later persuaded to return Chryseis to her father, but takes from Achilles his war prize Briseis. Achilles, enraged at this action withdraws his own, as well as the Myrmidons', participation from the war

Book Two: Zeus incites Agamemnon to attack Troy by sending him a dream messenger. Although certain war leaders disagree and seem determined to return home, they are finally persuaded to stay. Preparations begin for a new assault. The participating armies are described.

Book Three: It is decided that the fate of the war will rest on the outcome of single combat with Menelaus fighting for the Greek side and Paris for the Trojan. The encounter takes place. Paris is wounded but Aphrodite hides him within a cloud. Since neither the Trojans nor Greeks are able to find him, Agamemnon proclaims Menelaus the victor.

Book Four: The gods discuss the developments of the war. This is followed by a full-scale battle in which the gods also take part, while the war leaders engage in single combat. Apollo warns that Achilles is returning to the battle. Athena encourages the Achaeans.

Book Five: Diomedes, demonstrating his outstanding valor, defeats first Aeneas and then Ares. His valor is praised.

Book Six: As the battle continues Diomedes narrowly avoids facing an old friend. Hector encounters his wife Andromache who confides to him her deep fears for his fate, her own and that of their son Astyanax. After attempting to comfort her, a heavy-hearted Hector, accompanied by Paris, returns to the battle.

Book Seven: The battle continues. Hector challenges the Achaeans "to duel in bloody combat" and from amongst nine volunteers, Ajax the Telamonian draws the lot. The engagement ends in a draw and a cease-fire is agreed upon.

Book Eight: Upon orders from Zeus, the gods refrain from participating in the battle, which goes against the Achaeans. When Hera and Athena protest, Zeus explains that his aim is to provoke Achilles into returning to the field

Book Nine: A delegation attempts to soften Achilles' resolve but he announces that only the sight of Hector torching the Achaean ships and reaching the Myrmidon camp would make him return to the battlefield

Book Ten: Agamemnon and Menelaus inspect the garrison. Odysseus and Diomides arrest a Trojan spy.

Book Eleven: A bloody battle takes place. Agamemnon and many others are wounded. Achilles sends Patroclus to Nestor's tent for news.

Book Twelve: The Trojans have surrounded the fortifications that protect the Achaean ships. Many Trojans distinguish themselves for their valor. Despite Polydamas' warnings against proceeding further, Hector insists saying «Fight for your country, that is the best, the only omen».

Book Thirteen: The battle in the vicinity of the ships continues and the outcome remains inconclusive.

Book Fourteen: A discouraged Agamemnon suggests abandoning all effort and returning home. Hera however tricks Zeus into sleep and as a result the Achaeans, with Poseidon's help, succeed in repelling the Trojans. Ajax wounds Hector

Book Fifteen: Zeus awakens. Enraged he reprimands Hera and orders Apollo to aid the Trojans. The Trojans counterattack and in the ensuing encounter the casualties are heavy.

Book Sixteen: Achilles agrees to lend Patroclus his arms and to release his Myrmidons. Patroclus arms himself and drives back the Trojans but is killed by Hector.

Book Seventeen: A battle takes place over Patroclus' body. Hector succeeds in taking Achilles' arms off the dead body, but Menelaus and Meriones are able to transport the corpse to the Greek camp.

Book Eighteen: Achilles decides to rejoin the battle to avenge his comrade's death. Hephaestus fashions the most magnificent shield for Achilles.

Book Nineteen: Achilles dons his new armor and mounts his chariot. One of his horses turns to him and prophesies that he will die by the hand of a god not a man.

Book Twenty: Zeus permits the gods to reenter the fray. Achilles leads the Achaeans into battle, routs the Trojans and wounds Hector whom Apollo saves

Book Twenty-one: As the battle continues the Skamander River fills with corpses. The gods finally retire from the action. The Trojans manage to withdraw to the city.

Book Twenty-two: Hector remains behind in order to combat Achilles who kills him after a dramatic pursuit.

Book Twenty-three: Patroclus is buried and games are held in his honor

Book Twenty-four: The twenty-fourth book illustrates the spirit of human compassion. It describes Achilles relinquishing Hector's body to aged Priam and promising him a nine-day cease fire so his son may have an appropriate burial.

THE ODYSSEY

Book One: Athena urges Telemachus to confront Penelope's suitors as they have invaded Odysseus' palace against her will and are frittering away his riches.

Book Two: Telemachus summons a council and prepares to depart.

Book Three: Desiring news of his father, Telemachus first visits the palace of Nestor in Pylos.

Book Four: Telemachus then visits the palace of Menelaus in Sparta..

Book Five: Odysseus is on the island of the goddess Calypso who has kept him captive for years. She finally permits him to leave and helps him build a raft, but a storm strands him on the island of the Phaecians.

Book Six: Odysseys encounters Nausicaa, daughter of King Alcinous who had gone to wash her garments in the river. She takes him to her father's palace.

Book Seven: While Nausicaa returns to the palace Odysseus heads toward the city. Athena disguised as a young girl covers him with a cloud and takes him to the palace. Odysseus falls at the feet of the queen asking for her help. Arete asks him who he is, and he explains only what happened after his departure from Ogygia. Later he withdraws and goes to sleep.

Book Eight: The Phaeacians decide to meet together and arm a ship to take the foreigner to his homeland. A great feast follows in the palace. Odysseus is unable to hold back his tears. Alcinous asks him to reveal his identity and to tell of his adventures.

Book Nine: Odysseus begins to narrate his adventures that cover the next three books. He reveals his identity, describes his departure from Troy, his arrival in the land of the Lotus-Eaters and from there to the land of the Cyclops, where the incident took place with Polyphemus, son of Poseidon.

Book Ten: Being the adventures of Odysseus on the island of Aeolus, in the lands of the Laestrygonians and on the island realm of the sorceress Circe.

Book Eleven: Odysseus' visit to the lands of the Cimmerians and his descent, following Circe's suggestion, into Hades to consult Teiresias regarding the future.

Book Twelve: Odysseus narrates how he escaped the Sirens, as well as Scyla and Charybdis, how his comrades perished because they ate the holy cattle of the Sun and how, he, alone and shipwrecked, was washed up on Ogygia, where Calypso, who desired him as her husband, looked after for him..

Book Thirteen: Alcinous, moved by Odysseus' adventures gives him many rich gifts and sends him to Ithaca. The sailors leave him sleeping on the shore. When he awakens Athena informs him he is now home.

Book Fourteen: the faithful swineherd Eumaeus welcomes him to his dwelling.

Book Fifteen: Telemachus is also on Ithaca and, upon the goddess Athena's suggestion, goes to Eumaeus' dwelling.

Book Sixteen: Athena restores Odysseus to his true appearance and Telemachus recognizes his father.

Book Seventeen: After Athena disguises him as a beggar Odysseus goes to the palace where Argos, his faithful hound, recognizes him and immediately thereafter dies.

Book Eighteen: The beggar Irus challenges Odysseus. When the two beggars fight, Odysseus is the victor.

Book Nineteen: Penelope appears and speaks with the stranger. Odysseus narrates imaginary tales of his life and assures her that her husband will return soon. Her handmaiden Euryclea washes the stranger's feet and upon discovering an old wound recognizes him. He, however, asks her to keep his identity secret. Penelope announces to the suitors that she will wed the one who repeats Odysseus' feat of shooting an arrow through a line of axes.

Book Twenty: The night is full of suspense

Book Twenty-one: Odysseus takes part in the contest and he alone succeeds in shooting the target.

Book Twenty-two: Aided by Telemachus and two faithful slaves, Eumaeus and Philoetus, Odysseus slays the suitors and puts to death his unfaithful slaves as well.

Book Twenty-three: Euryclea announces the return of Odysseus to Penelope, but she has difficulty recognizing him. She is finally persuaded when he describes their bridal bed, which he had put together with his own hands. In the morning, Odysseus leaves the city to visit his father old Laertes.

Book Twenty-four: A recognition scene takes place on Laertes' farm in the country. The kin of the slain suitors desire revenge but Athena and Zeus intervene and the Ithacans are reconciled.

The great epic poet is crowned by Nike, in the presence of all the major historical and intellectual figures.
(Ingres, "Apotheosis of Homer", Louvre collection)

HESIOD

8th century BC

Major epic poet. His work, heralding as it did a rational scientific spirit, was considered prophetic. In contrast to Homer, who praised bravery and valor, Hesiod elected to deal with the world of simple poor folk and to offer counsel that would assist them in escaping fate.

ΟΥ ΜΕΝ ΓΑΡ ΤΙ
ΓΥΝΑΙΚΟΣ ΑΝΗΡ
ΛΗΙΖΕΤ᾽ΑΜΕΙΝΟΝ
ΤΗΣ ΑΓΑΘΗΣ, ΤΗΣ ΑΥΤΕ
ΚΑΚΗΣ ΟΥ ΡΙΓΙΟΝ ΑΛΛΟ

For a man wins nothing
better than a good wife,
and then again nothing
deadlier than a bad one.

ΔΙΚΗ Δ᾽ΥΠΕΡ
ΥΒΡΙΟΣ

Justice prevails over arrogance.

ΝΗ ΟΛΙΓΗΝ ΑΙΝΕΙΝ,
ΜΕΓΑΛΗ Δ᾽ΕΝ
ΦΟΡΤΙΑ ΘΕΣΘΑΙ

Praise the small ship
but put your cargo
on a large one.

ΤΟ ΕΡΓΑΖΕΣΘΑΙ
ΑΜΕΙΝΟΝ

It is best for one to work.

ΓΗ ΠΑΝΤΩΝ ΜΗΤΗΡ

The earth is mother to all.

His life

Hesiod was born in the village of Ascra in the Greek province of Boeotia, probably around the mid 8th century BC to a family originally from Cyme in Asia Minor. His father's involvement in shipping and marine transportation suggests that the family belonged to the nobility of the period. Having failed at his business, however, Hesiod's father moved the family to Ascra to a small farm on the slopes of Mount Helicon.

Upon the death of his father, the poet and his brother Persus, unable to agree on the division of the estate ended up in court. Persus however, who was not a sterling character, used bribery and other illegal means to appropriate Hesiod's portion. Later when Persus had succeeded in squandering the entire family fortune, he did not hesitate to request his brother's help. Hesiod refused him. This dispute later impelled him to compose *Works and Days*.

The death of this great poet is reported to have come about in this manner: After his victory in a poetry match in Chalkis, he dedicated his trophy to the temple at Delphi. There, a prophecy advised him to avoid the forest of Nemean Zeus, because he was fated to die. Hesiod, believing the prophecy referred to the place Nemea, went to Oinoi in Lokris, where there was a sanctuary of Nemean Zeus. He was subsequently murdered by the sons of his host King Figeas, who thought he had seduced their sister.

His work

When literary criticism sets out to evaluate Hesiod's times and work it does so in relation to Homer's. This is both truly necessary as well as useful since these two poets constitute, each one for his period, not only the most important source of literary material but also the only expression of that period's spirit and views.

Thus Homer, who predates Hesiod by at least one generation, deals in his poetry with proud and greathearted princes who, seeking fame and glory, fight alongside their people, with heroes of noble or divine birth, or with gods who neither change nor evolve.

Hesiod, on the contrary, came from a village in Boeotia and was interested in presenting the life of the simple poor people who inhabit a world of pain and anxiety, because they are trapped between anarchy and tyranny, serving many masters rather than one king; because although they have land, it does not provide them a sufficient living; because there is no solidarity, since neighbor turns against neighbor, friend against friend, and, as his personal experience showed, brother against brother.

Hesiod concluded that only hard work could rescue the poor from hunger and misery. He therefore did not deal with the past but, instead, scrutinized the world in which he lived with a positive eye. He tried to understand the life of his times and to better it with moral precepts. His aim was to teach not to entertain. Thus, while Homer was the poet of the heroic epic, Hesiod was considered the father of the didactic epic poem and proverbial philosophy.

Hesiod is reputed to have written a great deal -we find references to at least seventeen separate compositions- of which the most important are the *Theogony, Works and*

Days and the *Shield of Heracles.* His other works are the *Catalogue of Women, Melampodia,* the *Marriage of Ceyx,* the *Five Ages of the World, Astronomy,* the *Maxims of Cheiron,* the *Descent of Theseus to Hades, Aegimius,* and the *Idaean Dactyls.*

In chronological order, the *Theogony* (Genealogy of the Gods) comes first. The poem consists of 1,022 hexameters and is at the same time a theological work and a study of the universe and its origins, since he not only deals with the known gods (Zeus, Apollo, Athena, etc) but also with the natural elements (earth, sky, and stars) as well as with certain basic forces, moral and other, that affect human life such as enmity, zeal, polity, victory, etc.

Works and Days consists of 828 hexameters and is the most representative of all of Hesiod's works. It is to this poem that Hesiod owes his reputation as the creator of the didactic epic and as a poet of inspiration. His main themes: Labor-Justice-Rivalry.

In the *Shield of Heracles,* a poem consisting of 480 hexameters the main subject is Heracles' victory over Cygnus, son of Ares and Pyrene. The greater part of the poem (180 lines) is devoted to describing Heracles' shield, and, although a homage to Homer's description of Achilles' shield in the *Iliad,* it adheres to new artistic and philosophical demands. Hesiod, by presenting a horrific portrait of war, expresses his own attitude towards life as manifested by the triumph of the power of law, of peace, and of productive effort as embodied in Heracles against the dark forces of war and fear represented by Cygnus. The ancient Greeks recognized Hesiod's innovation from very early on and considered him the representative of a new genre of poetry, a prophet of the changing times, and a harbinger of the rational scientific spirit in contrast to Homer the bard of the old heroic world. Hesiod's work was esteemed as much as Homer's. Echoes of his views are found in Solon, Aeschylus, Pindar and other writers. It served as the model for Virgil's *Georgics.*

ΕΙΡΗΝΗ ΑΝΑ ΓΗΝ ΚΟΥΡΟΤΡΟΦΟΣ

Peace upon the land feeds man.

ARCHILOCHUS OF PAROS

725-680 BC

Lyric poet, renowned for the ironic
and satirical fashion with which he
did not hesitate to mock not only
events and his fellow man
but also himself.

ΘΕΟΙ ΑΝΗΚΕΣΤΟΙΣΙ ΚΑΚΟΙΣΙΝ ΕΠΙ ΚΡΑΤΕΡΗΝ
ΤΛΗΜΟΣΥΝΗΝ ΕΘΕΣΑΝ ΦΑΡΜΑΚΟΝ

God gave man great patience
to deal with incurable ills.

ΠΟΛΛ᾽ ΟΙΔ᾽ ΑΛΩΠΗΞ, ΕΧΙΝΟΣ ΔΕ ΕΝ ΜΕΓΑ

The fox knows many things, while the porcupine only one,
but its excellent.

Archilochean Dart

(In antiquity, the expression
Archilochean dart illustrated
the quality of Archilochus' satire
and came to denote any such
scathing comment.).

En Epigram

«Εις Μεγάτιμον και Αριστοφόωντα, Ναξίους Υψηλούς, Μεγάτιμον Αριστοφόωντά
τε Νάξου κίονας, ώ μεγάλη μαί υπένερθεν έχεις»

(Those high pillars of Naxos, Aristophon and Megatimos,
Oh great earth, you now cover.)

His life and work

Archilochus was a major poet who was considered Homer's equal. He is also the earliest of the Greek poets for whom biographical details survive. His father headed a colonial military expedition to the island of Thasos and Archilochus participated in some of the operations that took place there. He referred to himself as both poet and warrior. At one point he stated that, though a subject of lord Ares, he was also a servant of the Muses and knew their wonderful gift.

Archilochus' verse depicted the hard and bitter life of a soldier. Tradition has it that he was killed in a battle against the inhabitants of Naxos by an islander named Corax.

The ancient Greeks attributed elegies, epigrams and hymns to him. The poet however, owes his fame to the lyric satires he wrote in iambic verse. Unfortunately all that remain are fragments, the longest of which consists of only ten lines.

Archilochus' poetry is extremely personal. He not only wrote frequently of himself, but he did not hesitate to parody and laugh at his own actions. Revealing with unmatched immediacy the various turns of his tumultuous life, his verse mocked the accepted values of the heroic world, struck out ruthlessly at his enemies and illustrated moments of touching tenderness and raw sensuality. The style is lively and, unlike earlier epic poetry, sparsely embellished, with few adjectives and brief similes.

A hymn he composed to Heracles begins thus:

"Joyful greetings to you glorious victor
Greetings to you Heracles and to you Iolaus
-Brave warriors both".

An elegy Archilochus composed upon the death in a shipwreck of a brother-in-law and many other passengers from Paros contained the following couplet that did not meet with the moralizing Plutarch's approval.

"Lamentation will not cure my grief, nor will banquets and celebrations
Make it any greater".

ΟΥ ΤΙΣ ΑΙΔΟΙΟΣ ΜΕΤ᾽ΑΣΤΩΝ ΟΥΔΕ
ΠΕΡΙΦΗΜΟΣ ΘΑΝΩΝ ΓΙΓΝΕΤΑΙ
ΧΑΡΙΝ ΔΕ ΜΑΛΛΟΝ ΤΟΥ ΙΟΟΥ ΔΙΩΚΟΜΕΝ ΖΩΝΤΕΣ
ΕΤΙ ΚΑΚΙΣΤΑ Δ᾽ΑΙΕΙ ΤΩ ΘΑΝΟΝΤΙ ΓΙΓΝΕΤΑΙ

No one has ever profited from death. He became neither better known
or respected by others. Most likely the appreciation of the living relates to life.
When you die the worst thing is that you leave forever.

SAPPHO

640-568 BC

The most famous female lyric poet of the ancient Greek world and possibly the first woman poet in the world. Liveliness, intense emotion, passion and eroticism distinguish her poetry.

Ο ΜΕΝ ΚΑΛΟΣ ΟΣΣΟΝ
ΙΔΗΝ ΠΕΛΕΤΑΙ ΚΑΛΟΣ
Ο ΔΕ ΚΑΓΑΘΟΣ ΑΥΤΙΚΑ
ΚΥΣΤΕΡΟΝ ΕΣΣΕΤΑΙ

A handsome man is handsome
so long as he stands before you
but a kind man remains comely
later and forever.

ΑΛΛΑ ΤΙΣ ΟΥΚ ΕΜΜ
ΠΑΛΙΓΚΟΤΩΝ ΑΡΓΑΝ
ΑΛΛ ΑΒΑΚΗΝ ΤΑΝ
ΦΡΕΝ ΑΧΩ

I am not one of those
who feel rancor
I am gentle and the soul within
my breast knows no rage.

ΣΚΙΔΝΑΜΕΝΑΣ ΕΝ
ΣΤΗΘΕΣΙΝ ΟΡΓΑΣ
ΠΕΦΥΛΑΧΘΑΙ ΓΛΩΣΣΑΝ
ΜΑΨΥΛΑΚΑΝ

When the soul is disturbed
by rage, guard yourself from
a garrulous tongue.

ΠΛΟΥΤΟΣ ΑΝΕΥ ΑΡΕΤΑΣ
ΟΥΚ ΑΣΙΝΗΣ ΠΑΡΟΙΚΟΣ

Wealth without virtue is no safe neighbor.

Her life and work

Sappho is considered the best-known female lyric poet of the ancient Greek world and possibly the first female poet in the world. She was born in Ereso, on the island of Lesbos, and was a contemporary of the poets Stisichorus and Alcaeus, as well as of Pittacus, one of the Seven Wise Men of antiquity. Her friendship with Alcaeus is said to have been particularly close; it is possible they were lovers.

Sappho was descended from an aristocratic family of Lesbos and had three brothers. She married a rich merchant from the island of Naxos and had a daughter Cleïs, whom she praised in a poem:

> *"I have a beautiful daughter, who resembles a golden flower*
> *My beloved Cleïs.*
> *I wouldn't take all of Croesus' Lydia, in exchange for her.*
> *Nor the desired one (Mytilene) either".*

During the period 603–595 BC, political unrest forced Sappho to leave Mytilene (Lesbos) and take refuge in Sicily, where she stayed in Syracuse. Upon returning home, between 590 and 580 BC, she founded a school of music and poetry for girls and women, whom the social and political mores of the era condemned to ignorance. She taught music, poetry, dance and manners.

Her influence over her young friends and students was such that they loved her with true devotion. This gave rise to the accusation that Sappho indulged in homosexual love with her female students and other friends. Certain writers, however, claim that Sappho's relationship with her female circle of friends was purely pedagogical and educational. Be that as it may, these rumors were the foundation of the gibes found in the works of the comedy writers of that era, especially in Athens.

Sappho wrote erotic poetry, prayers and hymns to the gods, as well as *epithalamia* (wedding songs). Only around 650 verses of her poetry have been preserved from a body of work estimated to have been ten to twenty percent greater.

The Alexandrine grammarians divided her work into nine books according to poetic meter rather than subject.

Sappho's poetry is distinguished by its liveliness, directness, emotional warmth and passion. Sappho contrasts the virile concept inherent in masculine poetry with her personal poetic ideal, which is not centered on armies of cavalry, or men-at-arms or ships but on whatever a person may love.

No other ancient Greek writer of erotic poetry was able to achieve the level of tenderness Sappho expressed.

The ancient Greeks loved and admired Sappho. They called her *the nightingale of Lesbos*, the *tenth Muse* and *sister to the Graces*. Some even considered her work equal to Homer's. In the 4th century BC the inhabitants of Syracuse, enchanted by her poetry, erected a statue in her honor.

ALCAEUS
7th century BC.

"Virginal black-haired Sappho
Of the sweet smile
My tongue wants to speak to you
But is restrained by shame".

(Alcaeus to Sappho)

*The honeyed poet Alcaeus
on a 5th-century-BC vase, Munich,
National Collection of Antiquities
and Sculptures.*

His life and work

A major lyric poet who was born and died on Lesbos at an advanced age. Alcaeus was from a noble family, a fact that caused him to become involved in the political disputes of his homeland.

Supporting the aspirations to power of a particular aristocratic faction of Lesbos he headed a secret society that aimed at deposing the tyrant Myrsilus.

Alcaeus has been described as both poet and soldier, but also as a devoted adherent to a cause, who involved himself passionately in the political conflicts that tore his island apart. In his youth however, not all his military adventures were to his credit; during a war with Athens, in an attempt to save his life, he cast down his shield and fled the battle. He was exiled twice, once to Pyrra on Lesbos and once off the island during which it seems he visited several regions including Egypt. He returned to his city after being pardoned by the tyrant Pittacus and lived there until the end of his life.

The Alexandrine scholars gathered Alcaeus' poetic work into ten books. All in all, only about 200 excerpts remain. He wrote hymns to the gods, factional poems and poetry to be sung at symposia. The surviving fragments of Alcaeus' political poems demonstrate a genius for satire that equals Archilochus. None of his erotic poetry, most especially the poems inspired by the beautiful black-eyed dark-haired youth Lycos, has survived to our day. In Alcaeus' *Scolia*, or *Symposia*, or *Sympotica* poems, which Horace used as a model, we discover the jovial description of a friendly group that had for every season a specific reason and occasion to celebrate.

Alcaeus filled his work with images of the hazards of the Aegean Sea. Like other poets, Ibycus, Sappho, and even Anacreon, Alcaeus was also deeply affected by the sight of spring's effect on nature; his poetry brings to life a Greece where running water, trees and birds are still abundant.

ALCMAN
7th Century BC

*"Seven couches and again as many small tables
heaped with intoxicating bread kneaded with flax seeds
and with intoxicating bread kneaded with flax seeds and sesame
and amongst the wine cups, honey cakes for the youths..."*

(Description of a symposium scene)

His life and work

Alcman, who wrote lyric poetry, was born in Sardis in Asia Minor, lived in Sparta and died there at an extremely advanced age. He was responsible for the evolution of early lyric choral poetry into a body of literature. Alcman's Sparta was vastly different from the strict militaristic society it would become in later years. During the poet's creative period, the cultural centers of mainland Greece were Sparta and Corinth, not Athens.

Alcman was particularly celebrated for his erotic poetry, not all of which was necessarily based on personal experience. His work was collected into six books. Alcman also wrote music to accompany his verse. The songs were performed by a chorus, mainly of maidens rather than a singer, and were therefore known as *Parthenia* (Songs for Virgins). He himself played the *kithara* (a lyre-like instrument), but also used the *aulos* (precursor to the modern flute) saying that it harmonized well with the voices of children and girls. Referring to the expressive and joyous style of his music, he said aptly:

"I know the songs of the birds, the songs of all the birds".

The short surviving excerpts of his work leave us with the impression of a charming and simple poetic style, just slightly commonplace, and very far removed from the flame that is Sappho and the exaggeration that is Alcaeus. He does however distinguish himself with certain exceptional descriptions of nature, which evoke Hesiod.

*"The boulders, streams, valleys, mountaintops slumber
And those serpents the dark earth feeds,
The wild beasts, the swarming bees
The fish in the dark depths of the sea
And the flocks of broad-spanning birds, all sleep".*

The Alexandrine scholars' catalogue of lyric poets began with Alcman's name.

PINDAR
528-438 BC.

**The greatest lyric poet of antiquity
and the last representative
of ancient Greek poetry. He composed
choral odes of all types, but only his
Epinician, or Triumphal ones have survived
in full. His poetry… uses words with
exceptional expressivity.**

ΠΡΕΣΒΥΤΕΡΟΣ ΕΥΛΟΓΟΣ
The mature man
must be sensible.

ΤΟ ΠΕΠΡΩΜΕΝΟΝ ΦΥΓΕΙΝ ΑΔΥΝΑΤΟΝ
No man can escape his fate.

ΕΙΔΕ ΤΙΣ ΟΛΒΟΣ ΕΝ ΑΝΘΡΩΠΟΙΣΙΝ, ΑΝΕΥ ΚΑΜΑΤΟΥ ΟΥ ΦΑΙΝΕΤΑΙ
Man gains no happiness
without labour.

ΘΝΑΤΑ ΘΝΑΤΟΥΣΙ ΠΡΕΠΕΙ
The acts of man are fleeting.

Seventh Olympian Ode:
To Diagoras of Rhodes, victorious in boxing

Strophe

«As when someone takes a goblet, all golden, the most prized of his possessions, foaming with the dew of the vine from a generous hand, and makes a gift of it to his young son-in-law, welcoming him with a toast from one home to another, honoring the grace of the symposium and the new marriage-bond, and thereby, in the presence of his friends, makes him enviable for his harmonious marriage-bed

Antistrophe

too, sending to victorious men poured nectar, the gift of the Muses, the sweet fruit of my mind, I try to win the gods' favor for those men who were victors at Olympia and at Pytho. That man is prosperous, who is encompassed by good reports. Grace, which causes life to flourish, looks with favor now on one man, now on another, with both the sweet-singing lyre and the full-voiced notes of flutes».

His life and work

Pindar was born in Cynoscephalae, near Thebes and died suddenly in the theater of Argos. He learned music from his father, a flute player, and from the Athenians Agathocleas and Apollodorus. His instructor was the poetess Myrtis. The great fame he achieved during his life endured after his death. When Alexander the Great sacked Thebes he ordered his soldiers to respect Pindar's house and leave it intact.

Pindar distinguished himself in all types of lyric poetry. The *Epinician Odes* or *Epinician Hymns* (triumphal odes) are the only composition of his to survive intact. They are separated into four books, each of which is dedicated to one of the four great pan-Hellenic games: the *Olympian Odes* honoring the victors in the Olympic Games, the *Pythian Odes* honoring the victors in the Pythian Games, the *Nemean Odes* the victors of the Nemean games and the *Isthmian Odes* those of the Isthmian games. No more than extracts from other hymns, paeans, dithyrambs, parthenia, dancing songs, encomia (song of extravagant praise), and dirges have survived.

In the *Epinician Odes* Pindar reports the actual victory in a few brief dry words and devotes himself to praising the victor, and above all his own and his family's homeland. He did this because, descended as he was from a noble family, he believed that virtues were inheritable.

Pindar rises above the simple reality of the games. He praises wisdom, virtue and beauty using magnificent images of unparalleled expressiveness, in accordance with the ideals of Doric aristocratic thought.

The *Epinician Odes* constitute the largest single complete body of Greek choral composition to be read continually from classical antiquity to the current day His poetry, distinguished by its technical perfection is usually inspired by myths, either specific to a location or common to the whole of Greece. He would, however, divest the myth of what he considered secondary or useless elements. He would transform it into the ideal. Pindar's work is also philosophical. He sought order, discipline, justice, and virtue.

An extract from Pindar's *seventh Olympian ode* is cited at the head of this entry. This ode deals with the boxing victory of Diagoras of Rhodes in 464 BC in Olympia.

Diagoras was one of the best known and honored victors of the ancient Olympic Games. The tale that comes down to us describes him being carried on his sons' shoulders during a victory lap in honor of the fact that his three sons as well as his three grandsons were all also victorious in the games. The spectators cheered him exclaiming:

«Κάτθανε Διαγόρα· οὐκ εἰς Ὄλυμπον ἀναβήσει»,
which means:
*"Let your end come at last Diagoras;
do not seek to ascend Olympus (i.e., to become a god)".*

BACCHYLIDES OF CEOS
510-440 BC

His life and work

The Alexandrine Canon numbered Bacchylides among the nine greatest lyric poets. He was a nephew of the poet Simonides and practically contemporary to the poet Pindar, and is said to have been a good student of the former as well as a rival of the latter. We know little of his life. He may have lived at the court of the tyrant Hieron in Syracuse, for whom he composed epinicians and he may also have spent time exiled in the Peloponnese.

Up until the mid-19th century we had little information about Bacchylides' work, as only about 100 lines attributed to him had been preserved. In 1869 however, a papyrus came to light in Egypt with about one thousand complete, or almost complete, lines of his verse. Lately more extracts from other papyri were added to this material. From this we may conclude that Bacchilydes cultivated almost all the known types of lyric poetry.

His work has been divided into nine books, six of which contain sacred poetry, i.e. dithyrambs, paeans, hymns, prosodies, parthenia and dancing songs while the other three, titled *Epinicians, Love* and *Praises* contain secular poetry.

Bacchylides' poetry is characterized by its simple language and folk wisdom, yet it also contains narrative scenes of rare vitality. Often evaluations of Bacchylides' work compare it to that of Pindar.

The result of this comparison is, naturally, not in Bacchylides' favor, which is not to say that his merit as a poet is small, but although Bacchylides is unparalleled in his narrative ability and adept at small stratagems, he uses a less complex language and offers, in a pleasing fashion, the genial wisdom of everyday life. He does not, however, possess Pindar's capacity to delve deeply into the essence of values or to handle the structure and essence of poetry successfully. In response to Bacchylides' dubbing himself the "nightingale of Ceos" (today Kea) there exists an epigram from the *Palatine Anthology* that, rather aptly characterizes the elegant but rather verbose poetry of Bacchylides.

"Oh Pindar, holy mouth of the Muses,
Oh Bacchylides, garrulous Siren"

Two of Bacchylides' poems draw their inspiration from the myth of the Athenian hero Theseus. In the first he narrates how, in order to prove to King Minos of Crete that he was the son of Poseidon, Theseus threw himself into the sea and how he was received by Amphitrite and then returned safe and sound to the ship, marvelously clothed and crowned. Quite a few of the words Bacchylides utilizes are of his own invention. They are usually compound adjectives formed by combining two other adjectives: bronze-helmeted is an example.

Lyric poetry was always recited to the accompaniment of music.
A young woman plays the lute. Bas-relief (440 BC) from the famous Ludovisi Throne found in Rome.

ANACREON
570 BC-485 BC

A lyric poet of ancient Greece
who was considered
the most foremost poet of love,
wine and carefree living.
He wrote symposium poems,
capable of creating a happy,
high-spirited ambiance.

«I do not love him who next to the great
ewer drinks wine and sings of battle
and grief-bringing war, but rather him who,
combining the merry gifts of Aphrodite
and the muses, calls forth a desired joy».

«Now my temples and head are white,
happy youth has fled forever,
my teeth are old. There is little time
left for this sweet life. Therefore I mourn, often,
because I fear Tartarus, the depths
of Hades are horrible and descending calls
for great effort. And having once descended,
no one can rise up again».

His life and work

Anacreon, a lyric poet of ancient Greece, was born and died in the Ionian province of Teos in Asia Minor, opposite the island of Samos.

A celebrated poet in his youth, Anacreon was particularly renowned as a witty, boisterous womanizer, a natural consequence of growing up in Ionia during a period of prosperity and plenty. Polycrates, then the tyrant of Samos, invited him to his court along with other poets, where he quickly became Poycrates' trusted favorite and even wrote odes for him.

Polycrates was generous to Anacreon, strewing him with honors. As the story goes, when he first gave Anacreon five talents, the poet remained sleepless for two nights, not knowing what to do with his riches while simultaneously worrying that he would lose this immense sum. Until, on the third day, he returned the coins to the ruler ridding himself of the burden. After the death of Polycrates, invited by the tyrant Hipparchus, a scion of the Peisistratus dynasty, he went to the Athenian court. He may also have visited the court of the Aleuadae in Thessaly. He was an old man by the time he returned home, where he died at the age of 85.

Anacreon was considered the preeminent poet of love, wine and the carefree life. His poetry was divided into five books, three of which contained purely lyric poems, another elegies, while the last contained iambic poetry. Of this extensive body of work, only fragments survive.

He wrote his poems to be sung during *symposia* (feasts) and create a delightful atmosphere. The poet Anacreon invites you to participate in the joys of life, without ever becoming coarse.

> *"I wish to sing of tender love*
> *Crowned as his is with garlands of flowers*
> *It is he who rules the gods*
> *And tames mortals as well".*

In 5th century Athens, many were fascinated by the Ionian and Aeolian poets. Aristophanes, for example, wrote in the Thesmophoriazusae:

> *"Look at the famous Ibycus,*
> *at Anacreon of Teos, and at Alcaeus,*
> *who handled music so well;*
> *they wore head-bands and found pleasure*
> *in the lascivious dances of Ionia".*

His subjects are inspired by his life as a court poet, a refined lover of feasting, handsome youths, and beautiful girls. Love in short, but of a type that does not contain the extremely personal element and passion of Sappho or Alcaeus.

THEOCRITUS
300 - 260 BC

Ancient Greek poet who was
held to be the foremost
representative of pastoral poetry
and the first to write poems in the
new idyllic literary style, which
describes incidents of daily,
especially rural, life in an epic
and dramatic fashion.

*Silver tablet, the scene possible portrays Theocritus.
(St. Petersburg, Hermitage Museum).*

ΤΥΦΛΟΣ Δ' ΟΥΚ ΑΥΤΟΣ
Ο ΠΛΟΥΤΟΣ, ΑΛΛΑ ΚΑΙ ΑΦΡΟΝΤΙΣΤΟΣ ΕΡΩΣ

Carefree love is as blind as wealth.

The Ode of Thyrses

"[...] Thyrses. Wilt thou, goatherd, in the nymphs' name, wilt thou sit thee down here,
among the tamarisks, on this sloping knoll, and pipe while in this place I watch
thy flocks?
Goatherd. Nay, shepherd, it may not be; we may not pipe in the noontide. 'Tis Pan we
dread, who truly at this hour rests weary from the chase; and bitter of mood is he,
the keen wrath sitting ever at his nostrils. But, Thyrses, for that thou surely wert wont
to sing The Affliction of Daphnis, and hast most deeply meditated the pastoral muse,
come hither, and beneath yonder elm let us sit down, in face of Priapus and the fountain fairies
where is that resting-place of the shepherds, and where the oak trees are [...]"

His life and work

The poet Theocritus was born in Syracuse on the island of Sicily. We only have a few contradictory details about his life. He appears to have studied on the island of Cos, famous since Hippocrates for its school of medicine. From his student days there he maintained a friendship with an old classmate whose name, Nilaos, is often found in Theocritus' poetry.

Since literature was more to his liking than medicine, Theocritus went to Alexandria where he became a regular in poets' circles. It seems that Cos and Alexandria were the two locations other than Sicily, the third center of his intellectual activity, that Theocritus preferred as well as the only places in which he situates the action of his poems.

Theocritus may have been the son of the famous physician of Cos Praxagoras, whose writings often mentioned Galen, the second best known physician of antiquity after Hippocrates. It was therefore natural that Theocritus, in this circle of sages, should have acquired an exceptional education and culture from an early age. His education was supplemented when he joined the entourage of the famous poet of Cos, Philetas. Many of its members later also found fame as poets. The works attributed to Theocritus that have come done to us include 30 idylls, 22 epigrams, excerpts from a poem entitled *Berenice* and the small singular poem *Syrinx*.

The most famous of his idylls are: *Thyrses* in which the shepherd of the title sings the trials of the mythical Daphnes; the *Thalusia* that describes a harvest time walk in the countryside of Cos, a subject linked to reality and the life and character of the poet; and the idyll *Adoniazusae*, a short four-part comedy, which describes the adventures of two women of Syracuse Gorgo and Praxinoa. Theocritus, more than any other poet of his generation, avoided demonstrating extreme erudition in his poetry. With his sensitive natural style of expression he showed himself to be a master of his chosen style of poetry and equal to the great poets who came before him. Theocritus possessed the sensitivity of someone who lived in natural surroundings and the colors, sounds, movement and scents that characterize nature in the Mediterranean are illustrated in his poems. Hs work is full of images.

In the extract from *Thyrses* quoted previously, the countryman Thyrses and a goatherd have met amid their grazing flocks. Thyrses begs the goatherd to play his reed pipes. The latter, however, refuses responding that his strident voice might wake up the god Pan from his midday nap.

ΕΛΠΙΔΕΣ ΕΝ ΖΩΟΙΣΙΝ
ΑΝΕΛΠΙΣΤΟΙ ΔΕ ΘΑΝΟΝΤΕΣ

As long as we live, we hope.

CALLIMACHUS

310 - 240 BC

**A Greek poet and literary scholar who was born
in the Greek colony of Cyrene on the coast of Libya and died in Alexandria.
He was a prolific and extremely erudite writer. The private lives
of the reigning dynasty were his primary source of inspiration
and it can therefore be said that he wrote a type of political court poetry.**

ΔΙΧΟΣΤΑΣΙΗ ΤΡΩΕΙ ΓΕΝΟΣ

Discord destroys the race.

ΜΕΓΑ ΒΙΒΛΙΟΝ ΜΕΓΑ ΚΑΚΟΝ

A great book is like great evil.

His life and work

Callimachus was born in the Greek colony of Cyrene on the coast of Libya and died in
Alexandria. He is considered the most characteristic representative of the Alexandrian
style. He was the grandson of a Cyrenian general whose name he bore. In one of his
epigrams he also referred to himself as "Battiadae", possibly desiring to show that his
line of descent went as far back as Battus, the legendary founder of Cyrene. This could
also have simply been a nickname. A suggestion that his father's name was Battus is
unsubstantiated.

Upon first arriving in Alexandria as a young man he found employment as a child-
rens' tutor. Judging from his achievements he must, however, have also worked with a
great deal of stubborn perseverance at his education. His teacher is said to have been
Hermocrates of Iassus. He found work at the Museum of Alexandria where he volun-
teered to draw up a catalogue* in order to facilitate use of the library. He put together
120 books of tables (*Pinakes*), a task that took years to accomplish. He married the
daughter of a family from Syracuse.

It appears that throughout all the stages of his career, he remained attached to the court of Ptolemy II and to the Museum of Alexandria. He never traveled by sea. Information we have that he studied in Athens is most likely false. He was still active when Ptolemy Euergetes ("Benefactor") took the throne in 247/6 BC.

Callimachus, as previously mentioned, was a both prolific and erudite poet and literary scholar. His poetry is reputed to have filled 800 volumes. From this body of work enough material for one single volume has been salvaged. But thanks to a variety of fragments found on papyri or on wooden plaques, as well as some summaries on a papyrus discovered in 1934, we can arrive at a fairly clear picture of his work and talent. Aside from the 120 tables for the Alexandrian Library he also wrote the following works: *Aetia, the Lock of Berenice, Hecale, Ibys, Hymn to Zeus, Hymn to Apollo, Hymn to Artemis, Hymn to Delos, Hymn to the Baths of Pallas, Hymn to Demeter* and 63 epigrams. As the private lives of the reigning dynasty were his primary source of inspiration it can therefore be said that he wrote a type of political court poetry

Aetia: It is a long poem. While in a dream, the poet questions the Muses about the heroes, as well as the origin of many Greek celebrations and customs etc. The Muses' answers appear familiar and humorous. Far from the important classical subject matter, the poet narrates a series of anecdotal and folkloric details. For example, he ask the Muses:

> *"Why do we sacrifice on Paros to the Graces without flutes and garlands?*
> *Or How should we interpret sacrifices that take place with evil prayers?"*

Aetia also contains the beautiful love story of *Acontius and Cydippe*, which Ovid later retold.

The Lock of Berenice: In this elegy, Callimachus was inspired by the astronomer Conon's announcement of his discovery of a constellation in the heavens to which he had given the name *Berenice's Hair* (Coma Berenices) and described the following episode: In 247 BC, when Ptolemy III Euergetes ascended the throne, he had to leave Egypt immediately to attend to the Syrian war in the east. His young and beautiful wife Berenice swore that should her husband return unharmed, she would dedicate a plait of her hair to the gods. And so she did. When the lock disappeared from the temple, the court astronomer Conon identified it with the group of stars that are known today as *Coma Berenice*.

Hecale: In Hecale Callimachus assumes an epic tone for a short while so as to grant us a charming narration of a scarcely known episode from the exploits of Theseus: the hospitality and maternal tenderness he was shown by Hecale, a compassionate old village woman, somewhere in the fields of Attica.

---

* The Alexandrian Canon of lyric poets included: Alcaeus, Sappho, Anacreon, Alcman, Stesichorus, Ibycus, Simonides, Bacchylides and Pindar.

Tragedy, then, is an imitation of an action that is serious, complete, and of a certain magnitude; in language embellished with each kind of artistic ornament, the several kinds being found in separate parts of the play; in the form of action, not of narrative; through pity and fear effecting the proper purgation of these emotions (VI).

(*Definition of Tragedy*, *Aristotle*, *Poetics*, translation by S. H. Butcher)

The ancient theatre at Delphi.

AESCHYLUS

525 BC-456 BC

His tragedies Agamemnon, Choephoroi (Libation Bearers) and Eumenides (Furies) form the trilogy known as the Oresteia and are Aeschylus' most accomplished work. With Aeschylus, action enters the realm of tragedy as he improved the scenery,caused the chorus to move and personally composed the music for his plays. His writing is driven by great religious feeling and teaches the values of justice and prudence.

ΤΟ ΜΗΤ᾽ ΑΝΑΡΧΟΝ
ΜΗΤΕ ΔΕΣΠΟΤΟΥΜΕΝΟΝ
ΣΕΒΕΙ

Respect neither anarchy nor despotism.

ΔΕΙ ΣΩΦΡΩΝ
ΔΙΚΑΙΟΣ ΑΓΑΘΟΣ ΑΝΗΡ
ΣΙΓΑΝ Η ΛΑΛΕΙΝ
ΤΑ ΚΑΙΡΙΑ

The sensible, fair and good man must be silent, speaking only what is necessary.

Ο ΧΡΗΣΙΜ᾽ ΕΙΔΩΣ ΟΥΧ
Ο ΠΟΛΛΑ ΕΙΔΩΣ ΣΟΦΟΣ

He who knows a few useful things is wise.

ΟΥΚ ΑΝΔΡΟΣ
ΟΡΚΟΙ ΠΙΣΤΙΣ,
ΑΛΛΑ ΟΡΚΩΝ ΑΝΗΡ

It is not the oath that makes us believe the man, but the man the oath.

His life and work

Aeschylus was born in Eleusis and died in Gela in Sicily. A nobleman, he was a scion of the Codridus family, which claimed descent from Codrus, the heroic last king of Athens. His father was Euphorion and he had two brothers Ameneas and Cynaegerus. His two sons, Evaeon and Euphorion were also tragic poets.

He fought bravely during the Persian Wars at Marathon, where his brother Cynaegerus fell heroically in the line of duty, as well as at Salamis. There is little information about his education. It appears, however, that he knew Homer's work well.

His entire opus illustrates the brave and proud creed of the Marathon warrior. He is the preeminent representative of that pure and brave generation of Marathon fighters whose names, as Demosthenes wrote, were used by the Athenians to consecrate their oaths: "By those who fought at Marathon". In contrast to Pindar who celebrates athletes, this great tragedian celebrated the liberators of Greece. The poet's entire family was aflame with patriotism and bravery.

The manner of Aeschylus' death is exceedingly strange as legend has it that it was the result of an eagle dropping a tortoise onto his bald head (!).

Aeschylus took up poetry at a very early age and in 486 BC won first prize in drama contests in the yearly Athenian Dionysia festival competition. From that time on and until 468 BC he was always awarded the first prize. However, in 468 BC, Sophocles defeated him. After receiving an invitation from Hieron, the ruler of Syracuse, he went to Sicily. He returned to Athens and then traveled again to Syracuse where he died. Aeschylus wrote between 70–90 tragedies and satiric dramas, of which only seven have survived: *The Persians, Agamemnon, The Choephoroi, The Eumenides, Prometheus Bound, The Suppliants,* and *The Seven Against Thebes.* The tragedies *Agamemnon, Choephoroi* (Libation Bearers) and *Eumenides* (Furies) form the trilogy known as the *Oresteia.*

Brought up on Homer and a contemporary of the glorious struggles of Athens against the barbarians, Aeschylus' tragedies reflect the religious and national spirit of that heroic era. Using a simple structure and inspired by a great epic spirit, he presents great and violent passions on stage, using neither-complicated combinations of events, nor psychological subtleties. Impetuousness and pride distinguish his heroes who are always driven by great passions. The magnificence of his imagery and greatness of his concepts are unsurpassed. His sublime poetry overwhelmed his audience.

And finally, the innovations introduced by Aeschylus are as follows:

- He added a second actor to the drama, thus violating the theatrical convention according to which each work had just one actor and the chorus.
- He limited the chorus to 12 persons and changed its function.
- He taught his own choral movements and may have invented new steps.
- He added costumes and masks which were impressive even though they were not yet close to developed stage design.

THE WORKS OF AESCHYLUS

The Persians (472 BC): Regardless of how it is examined, this tragedy is one of a kind. Its subject is not some myth but the Greek victory at Salamis, an actual historical event not far removed from the time it was written. It is also, thanks to a shift in the point of view, not a triumphant explosion of patriotic enthusiasm but the study of a defeat. It is the defeated nation that is observing the event and the action takes place in the capital of Persia where the disaster is announced. The principal characters are suffering under the weight of anguish: Xerxes, the dead Darius, the Queen, the Senate advising the throne. In the entire play not one name is mentioned.

Nothing in this work stresses the pride of one or the other side. We are watching a downfall, which, as Aeschylus implies from start to finish in the play, is the outcome of a divine decision and constitutes the punishment of the Persians for the war waged a few years earlier against Greece.

The Seven Against Thebes (467 BC): The play presents the fratricidal struggle for the throne of Thebes waged by Oedipus' two sons, Eteocles and Polyneices. The philosopher Gorgias has described this piece as filled with war. The messenger reveals that Polyneices has declared war against his home and his brother. The chorus of Theban maidens is filled with fear at the news. Seven war leaders will each lead an assault against the seven Theban gates. Polyneices himself lays siege to the seventh gate that is defended by Eteocles. In the course of the battle both brothers are killed.

The governing body of Thebes decides that while Eteocles will be buried with honors, Polyneices' corpse will remain unburied, at the mercy of any wandering dog packs. Their sister Antigone's immediate reaction and her announcement that she will see her brother buried presage new catastrophes.

The Suppliants (463 BC?): The tragedy takes its subject from the myth of the Danaids, daughters of Danaus, who arrive as suppliants at the altars of Argos. They are pursued by the sons of the king of Egypt, whose wives they do not wish to be. Pelasgus, the King of Argos, becomes the central figure of the tragedy from the moment the suppliants request his assistance, as he is aware that his decision to come to their aid will cause war between his realm and Egypt.

Prometheus Bound (date uncertain): It is probable that the tragedy constituted the middle play of a trilogy that also included the tragedies Prometheus Fire Bearer and Prometheus Unbound. It describes the punishment of the Titan Prometheus who upon stealing fire from the heavens gave it to man and taught humankind all the trades as well. The central idea of the play is that any purpose that is either great or benefits humanity will lead to suffering. His treatment of Zeus, master of Olympus and exceedingly violent ruler of his domain, is striking.

Agamemnon (458 BC): The first tragedy belonging to the trilogy bearing the general title Oresteia, which narrates the disasters that struck the House of Atreides. Agamemnon, after the sack of Troy, returns to Argos with much war booty as well as Priam's daughter, the seeress Cassandra as his concubine. His wife Clytemnestra, who during his absence lived with Aegisthus, welcomes him with expressions of respect and love, as befits the victor in war. Cassandra, however, in a prophetic frenzy reveals to the chorus the murders that will follow. She and Agamemnon are slaughtered, and Clytemnestra and Aegisthus attempt to justify their crimes to the chorus.

The Choephoroi: The second tragedy of the trilogy. Orestes avenges his father's death, killing Aegisthus and his mother. But Orestes is maddened and with the terrible Erinyes (Furies) after him, he is forced to flee Argos.

The Eumenides: The action moves to the altar of Apollo in Delphi. Orestes is sitting there surrounded by the Erinyes. Upon the god's instructions he departs for Athens where he is to be tried for the murder of his mother. The goddess Athena sets up the Areopagus (high court) and later casts the vote that acquits Orestes. Appeased, the Furies become the Eumenides (Kindly Ones).

Terracotta mask used in ancient drama.

«Ὦι παῖδες Ἑλλήνων ἴτε
ἐλεθεροῦτε πατρίδ᾽ ἐλευθεροῦτε δέ
παῖδας, γυναῖκας θεῶν τε πατρώων ἕδη,
θήκας τε προγόνων νῦν ὑπέρ πάντων ἀγών».

"Advance, ye sons of Greece, from thraldom save
Your country, save your wives, your children save,
The temples of your gods, the sacred tomb
Where rest your honour'd ancestors; this day
The common cause of all demands your valour".

(From the "Persians", 402)

SOPHOCLES

496 -406 BC

**Major tragic poet of the 5th century BC.
The Athenian audiences responded
enthusiastically to his emergence
as his work was animated by serenity
and was therefore most appropriate
to meet the requirements of an audience
enjoying the triumphs of Athens.
He brought about many innovations
in the art of dramaturgy.**

ΕΝ ΤΟΙΣ ΓΑΡ ΟΙΚΕΙΟΣΙΝ
ΟΣΤΙΣ ΕΣΤΙ ΑΝΗΡ
ΧΡΗΣΤΟΣ ΦΑΝΕΙΤΑΙ ΚΑΝ
ΠΟΛΕΙ ΔΙΚΑΙΟΣ ΩΝ

Whoever who handles his own affairs
well, will prove to be a fair ruler.

ΕΣΤ᾽ ΕΛΠΙΣ
Η ΒΟΣΚΟΥΣΑ ΤΟΥΣ
ΠΟΛΛΟΥΣ ΒΡΟΤΩΝ

Hope is what sustains most people.

ΟΥΤΟΙ ΣΥΝΕΧΘΕΙΝ ΑΛΛΑ
ΣΥΜΦΙΛΕΙΝ ΕΦΥΝ

'Tis not my nature
to join in hating, but in loving.

ΣΤΕΡΓΕῚ ΓΑΡ ΟΥΔΕΙΣ
ΑΓΓΕΛΟΝ ΚΑΚΩΝ ΕΠΩΝ

No one loves the bearer
of bad news.

ΑΝΑΡΧΙΑΣ ΔΕ ΜΕΙΖΟΝ
ΟΥΚ ΕΣΤΙ ΚΑΚΟΝ

There is no worse evil than anarchy.

His life and work

Sophocles was born in the Athenian demos of Colonus. His father Sophillus was one of the wealthiest manufacturers in Athens. He manufactured weapons and filled city government orders. As a consequence Sophocles' character was both measured and conservative. As a youth Sophocles was admired for his athletic body and fair face. In 480, his beauty, his athletic achievements and his musical talent caused him to be selected to lead the chorus during the celebration of Xerxes' crushing defeat at the naval battle of Salamis.

He received an excellent education and from an early age would come first in musical and gymnastic contests. His musical education was so good that he composed the music for choruses of his tragedies. He studied the traditional epic and lyric poets well. Sociable and garrulous, he maintained good relations with all the intellectual and political personalities of his day: Pericles, Herodotus, etc.

His first wife was Nicostrate, with whom he had one son Iophon. Later, Nicostrate was succeeded by one of his lovers Theoris, who gave him a son, Ariston. This son, in his turn became the father of the younger Sophocles who staged *Oedipus at Colonus* after his grandfather's death. A man of outstanding grace and beauty, with a well-known talent for the guitar and dance, he is said to have enjoyed the company of courtesans, even at an advanced age. He lived for over ninety years. The Athenians so admired his poetry that they called him *Melissa* (i.e. Bee, an insect held by the Greeks in high esteem).

We have no substantiated information regarding the cause of his death. It is said that he choked on a grape, or that he died either of exhaustion after reading a large portion of the *Antigone*, or of excessive emotion upon learning of his victory in a drama contest.

It is estimated that Sophocles wrote 86 tragedies and 18 satiric dramas*. He also wrote elegies, paeans and an ode to the historian Herodotus. From his work, only seven tragedies and one unfinished satiric drama remain.

According to his biographers, Sophocles was victorious twenty-six times in drama contests and never placed below second.

He introduced many important innovations to the drama of his time. He abandoned the system of a trilogy or tetralogy of plays sharing a common theme and instead instituted an independent trilogy or tetralogy with no common link; he reduced the amount of lyric poetry and the grandiloquence that was a mark of Aeschylian drama. He increased the chorus members from 12 to 15, established backdrop painting, improved all aspects of the spectacle and increased the number of actors from two to three.

---

* Satiric drama: This is the third genre of ancient Greek drama. The name is derived from the chorus which was made up of people dressed as Satyrs. Satiric drama was played as the fourth work in a tetralogy after three tragedies, to provide rest for the spectators.

THE WORKS OF SOPHOCLES

Ajax: The earliest of Sophocles' dramas to have been preserved. The hero of the drama is overcome by rage because Achilles' arms went as an award for bravery to Odysseus rather than to him. When he recovers he commits suicide with a sword Hector had given him. Agamemnon forbids Teucrus to bury his dead brother. Odysseus then intervenes and achieves both Ajax's burial and the restoration of the dead hero's honor.

Antigone: The most famous of Sophocles' tragedies.
After the campaign against Thebes ends in the defeat of the armies of Argos, Creon the ruler of Thebes, forbids the burial of Polyneices, because he had taken up arms against his city. Antigone, sister to Polyneices and betrothed of Haemon, son of Creon, disobeys Creon's order and buries the dead man. Creon orders her put to death. The consequences of this action are the suicides of first Haemon and then of his mother Eurydice, Creon's wife. After all these events, Creon admits that his impiety has been punished.

The Trachiniae (Maidens of Trachis): Deianeira, the wife of Heracles, fearing that the beauty of the princess Iole would tempt Heracles, sends him a tunic dipped in the blood of the Centaur Nessus. When Heracles dons the tunic, terrible pains overcome him. Upon learning of Heracles' pain Deianeira commits suicide. Heracles' son leads him to the mountain of Oiti where he after being consumed on a pyre he will take his place amongst the immortals.

Oedipus Rex (Oedipus the King): Oedipus' efforts to uncover the murderer of the previous king, Laius, in order to rid the city of the plague ultimately lead him to discover that he is a patricide and that his wife Jocasta is also his mother. Jocasta commits suicide and Oedipus puts out his eyes.

Electra: After returning to Mycenae with his companion Pylades, Orestes, assisted by Electra, kills his mother Clytemnestra and Aegisthus, slayers of Agamemnon. The triumph of justice purifies this act of matricide.

Philoctetes: According to the Oracle's prophecy, in order to conquer Troy, the Greeks needed the bows of Heracles. These were in the hands of Philoctetes, who had been abandoned on Lemnos by the Greeks at the beginning of the military campaign. In the tenth year of the war, Odysseus and Neoptolemus are sent to persuade Philoctetes to come to Troy with his weapons. He refuses, but at one point falls into a frenzy and Neoptolemus takes his weapons. Odysseus asks Neoptolemus to surrender the bows to him. Instead Neoptolemus returns them to Philoctetes when he recovers.

Oedipus at Colonus: Oedipus wanders for many years after being exiled from Thebes by his sons and the citizens of Thebes. Only his daughters, Antigone and Ismene remain by his side. They arrive at the holy grove at Colonus. Theseus annoyed by Creon's demands to protect Thebes protects Oedipus instead. Oedipus departs from this world in a strange fashion. He apparently disappears into the earth of Colonus, where he will become a mysterious source of protection for the land where he found his last refuge.

Archaic copy of the Ionian school showing two men dancing to the double pipes

"...to the gods alone is given immunity from eld and death;
But nothing else escapes all-ruinous time.
Earth's might decays, the might of men decays,
Honor grows cold, dishonor flourishes,
There is no constancy 'twixt friend and friend,
Or city and city; be it soon or late,
Sweet turns to bitter, hate once more to love".

(*Oedipus at Colonus*, Translated by F. Storr)

ΕΡΩΣ ΑΝΙΚΑΤΕ ΜΑΧΑΝ
O love, thou art victor in battle.

EURIPIDES

480-407 BC

Euripides introduced the prologue
and the *deus ex machina*.
He also relegated the chorus
to the background of the action
and succeeded in increasing
the lyric and musical elements
of the play. In his subject matter,
Euripides appeared to abandon
the idealized figures of previous
playwrights. Characters such as that
the of courtesan (Helen) or the skinflint
(Bellerophon) ascended the stage
and with them came
all the humbleness as well
as the reality of everyday life.

ΑΝΑΓΚΗΣ ΟΥΔΕΝ
ΙΣΧΥΕΙ ΠΛΕΟΝ

Nothing is stronger than necessity.

ΟΛΒΙΟΣ ΟΣΤΙΣ ΤΗΣ
ΙΣΤΟΡΙΑΣ ΕΣΧΕ ΜΑΘΗΣΙΝ

Fortunate is he
who has studied history.

ΑΙ ΔΕΥΤΕΡΑΙ ΠΩΣ
ΦΡΟΝΤΙΔΕΣ ΣΟΦΩΤΕΡΑΙ

In this world second thoughts,
it seems, are best.

ΑΠΑΝΤΕΣ ΕΣΜΕΝ
ΕΙΣ ΤΟ ΝΟΥΘΕΤΕΙΝ ΣΟΦΟΙ

When we are giving advice,
we are all wise.

ΚΑΚΗΣ ΑΠ'ΑΡΧΗΣ
ΓΙΝΕΤΑΙ ΚΑΚΟΝ ΤΕΛΟΣ

A bad beginning
makes a bad ending.

ΔΕΙΛΟΙ Δ'ΕΙΣΙΝ
ΟΥΔΕΝ ΟΥΔΑΜΟΥ

Cowards are nothing everywhere.

His life

Euripides was born on Salamis and died while at the court of Archelaus, king of Macedonia and the patron of the arts.

If we trust the mocking allusions to the great poet's origins in the works of the comic poets of the time, his parents were poor and practised occupations considered degrading. His father was a small-time trader and his mother a vegetable-vendor.

Relief depicting Euripides seated. Istanbul Museum.

Whatever the truth may have been, it did not stop Euripides from acquiring an excellent education in both philosophy and science. His library was considered one of the most comprehensive private libraries in Athens. From youth he was honored with various offices, something attributed to his sober and energetic character as well as to his love of learning. He was also an athlete who distinguished himself in particular events.

Though of a philosophical disposition, Euripides preferred poetry to prose as a means of developing and promulgating through art his philosophical ideas and beliefs that differed in many ways from what he perceived around him. It is to this perhaps that we owe our impression of Euripides as a haughtily solitary man of letters, withdrawn from the world, scowling, melancholy and unsociable.

Expressing the contradictory spirit of his time, characterized by a passion for the logical analysis of institutions and values, as well as for the reevaluation of ideas, he used drama to express, among other things, his mistrust of religious tradition and the very essence of anthropocentric religion. Using psychological analysis he attempted to bring man face to face with himself and his problems. He conceived and expressed the tragic state of life as something that results from the conflict between individuals of different temperaments.

His work

Euripides wrote 92 dramas and 3 tetralogies of which 17 tragedies, a satiric drama and many extracts survive.

He wrote his first tragedy at 18, and won his first prize in the poetic contests in 442 BC. In the drama contests, Euripides was unlucky and was victorious only five times. Undoubtedly, Euripides, if not the greatest of the tragic poets, is certainly the most tragic, a writer whose theatrical art literally overcomes the audience.

THE WORKS OF EURIPIDES

Alcestis:

Admetus, only son of the king of Pherae in Thessaly is fated to die unless another sacrifices his life for him. While his elderly parents refuse to offer their lives, Admetus' young and beautiful wife Alcestis willingly gives up hers in order to save him. Heracles, however, seizes her from Hades and brings her back to life.

Medea:

Desirous of wedding Glauke, daughter of the king of Corinth, Jason abandons his wife Medea. But she sends Glauke an enchanted veil for her wedding, a gift that poisons the prospective bride. Then, to revenge herself upon Jason, Medea slaughters her own children and in a winged chariot escapes for Athens.

The Heracleidae (Children of Heracles):

Euripides attacks the ingratitude of Sparta and Argos towards Athens, because while Athens protected the children of Heracles, who were fleeing their murderous uncle Euristheus, the Spartans, descendants of Heracles, declared war against Athens. A patriotic play.

Hippolytus:

Hippolytus, son of Theseus honors the goddess of virginity Artemis by offering her a garland, thus scorning Aphrodite with this action. In revenge, she causes his stepmother, Phaedra, to fall in love with him. Hyppolytus rebuffs her love and Phaedra hangs herself out of shame, but leaves behind a letter in which she accuses Hyppolytus of attempting to rape her. Theseus believing this incident took place curses his son and expels him. Outside of Athens Hyppolytus is killed by Poseidon. At the end a deus ex machina, in the form of Artemis, reveals the truth to Theseus who breaks down, mourning the unjust loss of his son.

Andromache:

The division of the spoils of Troy has given Hector's widow, Andromache to Neoptolemus, son of Achilles. Neoptolemus' wife, Hermione and her father Menelaus plan the deaths of Andromache and her son. This murder is thwarted by Peleas, grandfather of Neoptolemus and father of Achilles. Menelaus departs for Sparta. Orestes, Hermione's former betrothed abducts her and kills Neoptolemus at Delphi. The tragedy's theme serves the politics of the time, as it is a searing satire of the cunning and arrogant ways of the Spartans.

Hecuba:

The sorely tried Queen of Troy, Hecuba, a prisoner of the Achaeans, sees her daughter sacrificed at the grave of Achilles, while the sea's waves wash up the body of her son, Polydorus, who had been murdered by Troy's false ally Polymestorus. In revenge Hecuba blinds Polymestorus and kills his children. An anti-war play, it demonstrates human suffering with immense power while condemning war and political expedience.

The Suppliants:

Seven Argive generals died in the battle against Thebes, but the Thebans will not allow them to be buried near their city walls. The mothers of the seven generals present themselves as suppliants to Theseus, king of Athens who defeats the Thebans and buries the Argive dead. This is a political drama that praises the Republic of Athens while reproaching Thebes. Its purpose was to raise Athenian morale. Here Athens is presented as the savior of Hellenism and of true piety, the city where free thought and democratic government originated.

The Madness of Heracles:

In part one, Lycus, King of Thebes, wants to kill the children of Heracles, who with their mother and grandfather have sought asylum at Zeus' altar. Heracles' unhoped-for arrival results in his saving his kinfolk and slaying Lycus. In part two, Hera, in an attempt to revenge herself on her unfaithful husband Zeus, sends madness to his son Heracles. In his madness he now slays those whom he had previously saved. Desperate he wishes to commit suicide. Salvation comes, not from the gods, but from man. Theseus persuades Heracles to live and continue to his struggles for the sake of humankind.

Ion:

At Delphi the Pythian Oracle is bringing up Ion, son of Creusa and Apollo. Creusa and her husband King Xuthus come to Delphi ask the oracle why they are childless. They take Ion back with them to their palace, an act that provokes Creusa's jealousy. Suspecting Ion is Xuthus' son from a previous marriage she tries to have him killed. Divine intervention saves Ion. Creusa is advised by the goddess Athena to reveal that he is her son, the result of her affair with Apollo. Ion becomes the acknowledged heir to the throne of Athens.

The Trojan Women:

This tragedy is influenced by the horrors of war. The abduction of the women of Troy, the slaughter of Polyxene, daughter of queen Hecuba, the death of young Astyanax and the sight of Troy burning evoke shocking sensations. With this play Aeschylus stripped the mythical victors of Troy of their glory and presented war as an arena where bestial ambition and man's destructive tendencies become apparent.

Electra:

Electra is living in a small hut in the countryside with her husband, the poor laborer from Mycenae whom her mother Clytemnestra married her to. Orestes comes to her and with her assistance slays Aegisthus and Clytemnestra, thus avenging the death of their father. The main subject of the play is matricide, an act so heinous that nothing can justify it.

Iphigenia in Tauris:

The goddess Artemis did not permit Iphigenia to be sacrificed at Aulis, but instead brought her to the land of the Taurae (Tauris: present day Crimea), where all strangers are sacrificed, as her priestess. The first stranger to arrive there is Iphegenia's brother Orestes, whom she does not recognise. The siblings' recognition scene is one of the most beautiful in the whole of literature. Orestes, fulfilling a prophecy of Apollo and aided by Pylades and Iphigenia, takes the cult statue of the goddess Artemis. Only thus, will he be able to rid himself of the terrible pursuit of the Furies who are hounding him for matricide. In their flight they risk being captured by Thoas, King of Tauris. The deus ex machina is Athena who intervenes and grants a happy ending. This is one of the loveliest of Aeschylus' plays. The lyrical parts are of an admirable perfection.

Helen:

A reflection of Helen, rather than the woman herself went to Troy. The real Helen was in Egypt. Menelaus arrives there; the couple recognizes each other and, because the king of Egypt Theoclymenus wishes to wed Helen by force, decide to flee the country. Using a sacrifice at sea as a pretext the couple succeeds in escaping. This is a romance in both in plot and atmosphere.

The Phoenician Women:

The longest of all the Greek tragedies (1776 lines) it takes its name from the women of Phoenicia who constitute the chorus. The subject is the same as Aeschylus' Seven against Thebes; it narrates practically the entire Theban war and the myth of the Labdacidae. A mythic history of Thebes in succeeding images, a collection of pure myths.

Orestes:

The subject is Orestes' fate after committing matricide. As Electra and Pylades are devotedly taking care of an insane Orestes, the Argives, in an effort to punish the matricide, lay siege to the palace. Menelaus intervenes to save his brother's son. Then Apollo intervenes and brings about a happy ending.

Iphigenia At Aulis:

The play is considered one of the poet's most accomplished. In order for the Achaean fleet to set sail from Aulis to Troy, Iphigenia, daughter of Agamemnon, must be sacrificed. Odysseus dupes Iphigenia into coming to Aulis by claiming that a marriage has been arranged between her and Achilles. But when the truth is reveled Iphigenia weeps and begs. In the end, however, this passive and weak creature becomes a proud and decisive personality that is elevated to become the symbol of the success of this great enterprise. At the very moment of the sacrifice, the goddess Artemis intervenes and, invisible, seizes Iphigenia and sends her to Tauris. In her place, she leaves a deer.

The Bacchae (Bacchantes):

King Pentheus of Thebes is attempting to prevent the introduction of the worship of Dionysus (Bacchus) to Thebes, but is devoured by the maddened Bacchae (followers of Dionysus) led by his mother Agave. Agave then dances maniacally holding the head of her son, thinking it the head of a lion. When she recovers she realizes the depths of the disaster. Dionysus appears in all his glory, pronounces the destruction of all those who condemned him and triumphantly ascends into the heavens. This is Euripides' best-constructed tragedy. It presents with impressive thoroughness the tragic conflict between the individual desirous of comporting himself according to the rules of logic and the realm of the illogic ecstatic element.

In his extensive work, Euripides introduced innovations in both in the dialogue and the choral segments of his tragedies. In tragedy's lyric segments his innovations consisted of decreasing the choral and increasing the actors' solo sections.

Terracotta mask dating from the 4th century BC and discovered at Tarentum (Taranto today).

«Τοῖς μέν γάρ παιδαρίοισιν ἔστι διδάσκαλος ὅστις φράζει,
τοῖσιν δ᾽ ἡβῶσι ποιηταί.
Πάνυ δή δεῖ χρηστά λέγειν ἡμᾶς».

meaning:

*"For boys a teacher at school is found,
but we poets are teachers of men.
We are bound things honest and pure to speak".*

(Aristophanes, *Frogs*)

ARISTOPHANES

446-385 BC

The greatest comic poet of antiquity.
His scathing work mocks
the excesses of corrupt state
officials, of sycophants,
and of embezzlers, attacking anyone
who took advantage of political life
for personal gain. He also deplored
war and moral corruption.

ΔΕΙ ΓΑΡ ΤΟΝ ΠΟΙΗΤΗΝ
ΩΦΕΛΕΙΝ

The poet must do good.

ΑΛΛ᾽ ΑΠ᾽ ΕΧΘΡΩΝ ΔΗΤΑ
ΠΟΛΛΑ ΜΑΝΘΑΝΟΥΣΙΝ
ΟΙ ΣΟΦΟΙ

The wise learn many
things from their enemies.

ΠΛΟΥΤΗΣΑΝΤΕΣ ΑΠΟ
ΤΩΝ ΚΟΙΝΩΝ ΠΑΡΑΧΡΗΜΑ
ΑΔΙΚΟΙ ΓΕΓΕΝΗΝΤΑΙ
ΕΠΙΒΟΥΛΕΥΟΥΣΙ ΤΕ ΤΩ
ΠΛΗΘΕΙ ΚΑΙ ΤΩ ΔΗΜΩ

Those who get rich from
the administration of public affairs,
become immediately unjust,
they scheme and fight
against the people.

ΟΥΔΕΝ ΕΣΤΙ
ΘΗΡΙΟΝ ΓΥΝΑΙΚΟΣ
ΑΜΑΧΩΤΕΡΟΝ

There is no worse beast than a
woman.

ΜΑΚΑΡΙΟΣ ΑΝΗΡ ΕΧΕΝ ΞΥΝΕΣΙΝ
ΗΚΡΙΒΩΜΕΝΗΝ

The happy man is he who has wisdom.

His life

Aristophanes is the greatest comic poet of antiquity and the most illustrious representative of ancient Attic comedy. His are the only comedies to have survived intact. We know little about Aristophanes's life. He was the son of Philip from the township of Cydathenaeum. His own birthplace was a matter of some dispute among his contemporaries. Some claimed that he was born in either Lindos or Camiros on Rhodes, others in Naucrate in Egypt, and yet others in Aegina. These disputes arose from unsubstantiated information claiming that the demagogue Cleon had accused Aristophanes of being foreign and usurping the rights of a citizen of Athens. It is, however, certain that Aristophanes spent the majority of his time on Aegina, where he owned land. These estates had been given to his father at the time that land claimants from Athens had moved to the island. He had three sons, Philip, Ararotus, and Nicostratus. The latter two seem to have been writers of comedies. In his private life, Aristophanes was characterised by exemplary dignity and consistent adherence to his principles.

It seems that Aristophanes' political and social beliefs tended towards conservatism and the tenets of the aristocratic faction, as his comedies abound in gibes against the democratic faction. This does not, of course, mean that he believed in oligarchy. He simply criticized the excesses of all unworthy representatives of the democracy of Athens, corrupt state officials, slanderers, embezzlers, and any politicians whom money could buy. He was a friend of peace. He hated civil war and the consequent poverty, devastation, and death. But the moral corruption and the depravity of politicians who had linked their personal advantage to the perpetuation of war enraged him most of all.

His work

Aristophanes probably wrote over forty comedies. Today we know the titles of 37 of his comedies, of which only 11 have been preserved. They are divided into three categories: 1) The political, into which category fall *Knights*, *Wasps*, *Acharnians*, *Lysistrata* and *Peace*. 2) The social, *Ecclesiazusae*, *Plutus*, and *Clouds*. 3), those that can be termed literary, which include *Thesmophoriazusae*, *Frogs*, and *Birds*.

Aristophanes was honored with a wreath of holy olive and was greatly esteemed. Even the King of Persia is said to have advised the Spartans to find an adviser of Aristophanes' caliber.

Aristophanes, as we can see from the subjects of his comedies, was interested in almost all of the issues of his time. His comedies are a valuable addition to the historical record, because they illustrate, better than anything else the daily life of his Athenian contemporaries, both urban and rural.

If the purpose of history is to reanimate past lives, the comedies of Aristophanes succeed in the best and most direct fashion.

THE WORKS OF ARISTOPHANES

Acharnians: We find ourselves in the sixth year of the war between Athens and Sparta and such are the disasters and the hatred between the combatants that all indications are that the war will perpetuate itself. In this atmosphere of hate, a great deal of courage is necessary in order to link the concept of Sparta and peace before an enraged populace. Only a poet could attempt to use laughter to mollify passion and direct the people's rage against those responsible for the war. Aristophanes, in the Acharnians becomes a public prosecutor and attempts to call forth his audience's disapproval of the corruption of the slippery politicians and warmongers in public office.

Knights: This comedy mocks the demagogue Cleon. The poet accuses Cleon and his entourage of profiting personally from public office and warns him that the patience of the people has its limits and that the disadvantaged will turn against their exploiters. At the same time he also attacks the Athenians, exposing them as easy marks for venal flatterers and calls upon them to change their ways.

Clouds: This is a biting satire of the Sophists. Aristophanes, in common with all conservative Athenians, considered the Sophists to be disrupters of society, godless charlatans and demagogues, individuals who succeeded in making wrong seem right, lies to appear as truth, etc. Socrates, because of his appearance and misunderstood teachings is the main target of the satire in the Clouds.

Wasps: Here he mocks the Athenian passion for litigation. Athens did not have professional judges. Every citizen who had completed his 30th year and had full political rights could enter the lottery that selected the judges. Aristophanes examines whether the judges of the Heliaea are truly independent, as the demagogues declare, or whether they are the demagogues' subservient lackeys.

Peace: This play reproaches the Greeks for their pro-war and meddling stance, while praising peace and the virtues that come as a consequence. The Athenian Cleon and the Spartan Brasidas, the two most rabid warmongers of the conflict were killed in the field of battle in the fall of 422. After this event peace negotiations began and continued into the spring. Peace was simply a matter of good will on both sides. All that was needed was a small impetus. It was this impetus that Aristophanes was seeking provide with this comedy.

Birds: This comedy is unique in Aristophanes body of work. It presents special historical interest as it may be considered a precursor of utopian literature. It not only satirizes various theories of political systems but demagogues and slanderers as well.

Thesmophoriazusae: A «woman's» play, it deals, as does the Frogs, with literary subjects and satirizes Euripides' misogyny by parodying certain scenes from his works

Lysistrata: The subject of this comedy is Panhellenic peace. The poet appeals to the Athenians and the Spartans to make peace and end the fratricidal war. Aristophanes addresses himself not to the men but to the women who are yearning for their husbands away at war for years. In this comedy the poet's use of a young and beautiful woman as the central figure introduces a new element.

Frogs: In this purely literary comedy Aristophanes criticises the works of the two great tragic poets, Aeschylus and Euripides, and attempts to show the audience which of the two aided or harmed Athens. In the end, Aristophanes' satire succeeds in totally condemning Euripides, characterizing him as a lesser poet and praising Aeschylus.

Ecclesiazusae: This is the third «woman's» comedy after Lysistrata and the Thesmophoriazusae. Here Aristophanes satirizes the Platonic ideas of female emancipation and free love.

Plutus (Wealth): This play protests against the unjust allocation of wealth and the inequality of social class.

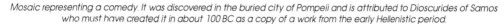

Mosaic representing a comedy. It was discovered in the buried city of Pompeii and is attributed to Dioscurides of Samos who must have created it in about 100 BC as a copy of a work from the early Hellenistic period.

Α ΨΕΓΟΜΕΝ ΤΑΥΤΑ
ΜΗ ΜΙΜΩΜΕΘΑ

What we deplore,
we should not imitate.

ΟΝ ΟΙ ΘΕΟΙ ΦΙΛΟΥΣΙΝ
ΑΠΟΘΝΗΣΚΕΙ ΝΕΟΣ

Whoever the gods love dies young.

ΟΥΔΕΙΣ ΕΠΛΟΥΤΗΣΕ
ΤΑΧΕΩΣ ΔΙΚΑΙΟΣ ΩΝ

No just man ever became rich all at once.

ΑΝΔΡΟΣ ΧΑΡΑΚΤΗΡ
ΕΚ ΛΟΓΟΥ ΓΝΩΡΙΖΕΤΑΙ

A man's character shows in his discourse.

MENANDER

342-290 BC

**Major Athenian poet and comedy writer,
styled "Star of the New Attic Comedy"
because he was the style's
primary representative.
He wrote a total of 108 comedies
and many one-line aphorisms.
Of his comedies, only one survives
complete ("Dyskolos")
and three almost complete.**

ΟΡΓΗ ΦΙΛΟΥΝΤΩΝ
ΟΛΙΓΟΝ ΙΣΧΥΕΙ ΧΡΟΝΟΝ

Anger against a loved one is short-lived.

ΦΟΒΟΥ ΤΟ ΓΗΡΑΣ·
ΟΥ ΓΑΡ ΕΡΧΕΤΑΙ ΜΟΝΟΝ

Fear old age,
it does not come alone.

ΙΣΧΥΡΟΝ ΟΧΛΟΣ ΕΣΤΙΝ
ΟΥΚ ΕΧΕΙ ΔΕ ΝΟΥΝ

The mob has great power but is not guided by the mind.

His life and work

Menander came from a rich family in Kifissia, suburb of Athens, and his parents Diopeithes and Hegisistrate took care to educate their child well. His talent for dramaturgy appeared very early. As a youth he studied with Theophrastus, at the time head of the Peripatetic school of philosophy established by Aristotle. He was a friend of the philosopher Epicurus and it so happened that they served their term of military service together. He loved the city of Athens, but lived in the country, near Piraeus with his beloved, the courtesan Glycera, who remained absolutely faithful to him. Ptolemy I repeatedly invited Menander to Alexandria. The poet, however, refused to leave the Athenians and the free intellectual life of Hellenistic Athens behind; it is also possible that he did not want to separate himself from his life's companion, the lovely Glycera.

Menander wrote 108 comedies of which four have been preserved intact while fragments remain of others. An anthology of one-line aphorisms was also preserved. Menander was renowned as a great composer of poetic aphorisms It transpired that these particular epigrammatic verses of his were collected early on, along with a number of other aphorisms in a special collection. Menander is unsurpassed in delineating the moral traits of his characters and is described as a "cutting, yet enormously affectionate observer of human stupidity and distress".

The Curmudgeon: The rustic god Pan appreciates the veneration shown him by the virtuous daughter of the curmudgeonly villager Cnemon and therefore induces Sostratus, an aristocratic city dweller, to fall in love with her. The crotchety, practically misanthropic Cnemon, however, does not even want to hear about such a wedding. So Menander creates a situation where Cnemon's associates devise a ploy through which after Cnemon falls into a well, Sostratus and his friends save him. After this, the course of events unfolds smoothly.

The Arbitration: The shepherd Daus finds a baby exposed in the wild with some jewels in its swaddling cloths. He gives the baby to the charcoal maker Syriscus to bring up but wants to keep the jewels for himself. They ask Smicrinus, an elderly man passing by to resolve the matter. Onesimus, a slave who chances to be passing by, recognizes one of the jewels as belonging to his master Charisius, The identity of the child is thus established.

The Rape of the Ringlets: The comedy's subject deals with the fate of the Corinthian merchant Pataicus' children, the twins Glycera and Moschion, who after being exposed in the wild are ultimately reunited with their father and everyone lives happily ever after. The title of the comedy comes from an episode in the play when, in a moment of frenzy, Glycera's betrothed Polemon cuts off her hair.

The Samian: The story of the love of Moschion, stepson of the rich Demeus, for Plangona, daughter of the poor Nicaretus and the fate of their child. The comedy takes its name from Chrysis, Demeus' wife who came from the island of Samos

Other comedies that Menander wrote but have not been preserved are the following: *The Woman-Hater, Nauclerus, The Twice Deceived, The Guitar Player, The Farmer, Perianthia, The Hero and Rage.*

The Parthenon.

PHIDIAS

490-432 BC

Considered the most brilliant
and famous sculptor of
Ancient Greece. His name
is linked primarily with
the Golden Age of Pericles,
during which Phidias
was inspired to create
great and prestigious works,
the Parthenon being a prime
example. In the work
of Phidias, Greek art found
its most perfect expression.

*Artemis, a detail from the Panathenaic Procession on the
Parthenon frieze, 447–432 BC, Acropolis Museum, Athens.*

Phidias and the Parthenon Frieze, Sir Lawrence Alma-Tadema, 1868.

His life

Despite an immense amount of information on Phidias' work, there is a lack of sufficient and accurate information on his life. Judging from his sculpture, however, we can place the pinnacle of his career during the period 470-430 BC. The son of the Athenian citizen Charmides and a relative of the painter Panaenus, Phidias demonstrated a great aptitude for painting. Nevertheless he devoted himself to sculpture and under the tutelage of either Hegias or the sculptor Agelades of Argos acquired an unmatched technique. He used wood, marble, gold, ivory, and bronze. It has been said that Phidias is to classical art what Pericles is to Athenian democracy. His personality stamped his era with his genius.

His work

Among the early works Phidias created are: a gold and ivory statue of the goddess Athena for the city of Pallene* of which no copy exists, a statue of *Apollo Parnopius* (persecutor of locusts) erected on the Acropolis of Athens; a bust of the poet Anacreon, a copy of which exists in the Copenhagen Museum and the great and magnificent statue of *Athena Promachos* erected on the Acropolis near the Propylaea. The gold-plated tip of Athena's spear was said to have been visible from Cape Sounion. War prizes from the battle of Marathon were used to create the statue.

Another of Phidias' early works was the *Athena Lemnia*, a bronze statue of the goddess dedicated by the Athenian claim holders of Lemnos that stood on the Acropolis. The bronze busts of famous heroes of Attica dedicated at Delphi, and, above all, the gold and ivory statue of Zeus at Olympia are also estimated to date from that same period immediately preceding his most creative one. The latter statue was a huge portrayal of Zeus sitting on a throne, decorated with painted decoration of precious metals and ivory. The height of the statue together with its base measured 12 meters; its head nearly touched the temple ceiling, giving the impression that should Zeus rise, he would take it with him.

Legend has it that when Phidias was asked what he would use as the model for the statue of Zeus, he retorted that he would use Homer's description of Zeus in the Iliad as his guide. "And Zeus, the son of Cronus bowed his craggy dark brows and the deathless locks came pouring down from the thunderhead of the great immortal king and giant shock waves spread through all Olympus". Then, after 448 BC came the period of Phidias' most sublime artistic achievements, when Pericles invited his collaboration in the execution of his great design for the artistic decoration of the Acropolis and in particular the Parthenon, temple of the goddess Athena.

His relations with Pericles and the political and intellectual circle, which had grown around him, lent a singular luster to the person of Phidias, revealing him as a figure of unique intellect and artistry.

---

*Pallene: a city of Achaea, whose harbor city was Xylocastro.

His name is closely associated with what has come to be called the *Golden Age,* because Phidias had assumed the responsibility for the supervision and management of all the projects that comprised part of a broad program of reconstructing the temples destroyed by the Persians during their invasion of Greece, as well as erecting many other monuments on the Acropolis, in Athens and in Attica.

Of all the monuments constructed during that period, the greatest was the Parthenon, the great Doric temple of Athena Parthenos erected on the Acropolis. This unique masterpiece was complemented by celebrated pieces of sculpture, which, created by Phidias' students and assistants, and by the master himself are all indubitably a product of his inspiration and spirit. Such works are the building's metopes depicting scenes from the Trojan War, from the battle of the Athenians with the Amazons, and from the struggle of the Lapiths against the Centaurs as well as scenes from the battle of the gods of Olympus against the Giants, the 'Gigantomachy'.

The Parthenon frieze is another such work. One meter high and 160 meters long, it depicts the Panathenaic procession. A total of 360 human figures and a multitude of animals comprise the frieze of the Panathenaic procession. Portrayed are gods, priests, noblemen, musicians, riders, riders, priestesses holding urns and canisters, old men holding branches, citizens of Athens, men, women, and youths as well as horses, oxen and rams.

The two pediments and their sculpted decoration, the final part of the construction work on the Parthenon, required five years to complete and are also the work of Phidias. In total more than 50 figures comprise the two compositions and the subjects are taken from the goddess Athena's mythology.

However, among the sculptures assembled in this universal shrine to art, the masterpiece was truly the chryselephantine (gold and ivory) statue of the goddess Athena, this too a work of Phidias. It rose to a height of 12 feet and stood, richly decorated, in the inner part of the temple. The statue's skeleton was made of wood; all exposed parts were of ivory, while the hair, gown and armament of the goddess were all made of gold. However, before the work on the Parthenon had been completed, Phidias -a victim of his friendship with Pericles, whom a constantly growing opposition was attempting to overthrow- was forced to flee Athens. First Pericles' opponents accused Phidias of having kept for himself a portion of the gold that the state had entrusted to him. Phidias, however, as if he had foreseen such a possibility had made the golden sections of the statue removable. He therefore took the pieces and weighed them before his accusers, thus providing indisputable evidence of his innocence.

A short while later he was accused of sacrilege, as he had supposedly caused the portrait of Pericles as well his own to be placed amongst the engravings on Athena's shield. His enemies succeeded that time in having him condemned and thrown into prison. Aided by friends he escaped and went into voluntary exile in Olympia, where he had created, as mentioned above, the statue of Zeus, a model of harmony and stateliness that was considered one of the Seven Wonders of the World.

Details from the Parthenon frieze 447–432 BC Acropolis Museum, Athens; Top: Urn Bearers, bottom: Riders.

POLYCLITUS

5th century BC

His life and work

Polyclitus worked primarily in bronze, and was one of the three great sculptors of the 5th century BC. Phidias and Myron were the other two.

He was the son of the sculptor Patrocleus, and his most creative period is placed around 460–420 BC. The great sculptor Ageladas of Argos taught him as well as Phidias and Myron. Polyclitus retained his studio in Argos although he worked in other locations.

Polyclitus is considered one of the foremost representatives of mature classical art. He was a restless spirit who delved into matters of artistic theory; proof of this inquiry was the study he produced on the ideal proportions of the male form. His book, entitled *Canon* was something of an artistic manifesto, the *rule* of ideal proportions.

He himself put into practice the theories his *Canon* set out in his famous *Doryphorus* (Spear-bearer), which, in fact, was also known as *Canon*. This statue depicts a young athlete holding either a spear or a javelin.

The Doryphorus of Polyclitus.
Roman copy of a Greek original,
440 BC. National Archaeological Museum, Naples.

The body is healthy with the right leg slightly extended while the left leg is bent and scarcely touches the ground.

This depiction of the young athletic male nude is usually the main form through which the ancient Greek artist's interest in plasticity is worked out. Here the subject may be the ideal Greek hero Achilles. Although this statue has been lost, many copies exist.

Among them are the statue of the *Diadumenus*, a youth binding a fillet around his brow and the figure of an *Amazon*.

The *Diadumenus* is one of Polyclitus' final pieces and exhibits many similarities to the *Doryphorus*. Its creation date is estimated to be around 440 BC and here too only a copy exists. A young victorious athlete is binding the victor's fillet around his brow. The form shows more pronounced movement. To the ancient writers this work portrayed a gentle tender youth in contrast to the *Doryphorus*, who was dubbed a virile young man. Pliny mentioned the *Amazon*, in reference to some sort of contest that took place for a statue of a bronze Amazon that was to be dedicated at the Temple of Artemis in Ephesus. The most renowned sculptors of the 5th century took part and Polyclitus was the victor.

Throughout the 4th century BC. Polyclitus' influence on a broad circle of students was evident. The large number of extant copies of his work dating from the Roman era also testifies to the breadth of his influence.

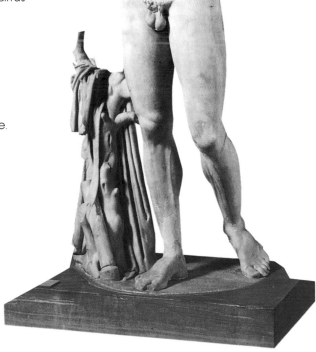

The Diadumenus of Polyclitus.
Copy of a Greek original, 430 BC. National Archaeological Museum, Athens.

PAEONIUS
5th century BC

His life and work

A sculptor from Mende in Chalcidice, The most significant of his extant works is the Olympia Museum's *Winged Nike* (Victory), which most probably dates from 425 BC. This statue, considered the finest rendition of a figure in flight is an outstanding work that stands on a triangular base and reaches a height of 9 meters. A fragment of the base remains inscribed with a dedication from the citizens of Messenia and Naupactos who had dedicated the work to Zeus on the occasion of their victory, along with their allies Athens, against Sparta. This *Nike* is depicted as she is flying towards the ground, her wings open and her clothing moving in the wind. It is a daring image of the winged goddess who, gliding through the air, seems to just touch the ground with her foot. Spreading her wings, she holds in her left hand a light Doric himation, while the tunic that clings to her maiden's body, bares her left breast and leg. This daring composition and the transparency of the Nike's garment presage the sumptuous style of the late classical era. This unique depiction, the *Paeonius Nike* has, to this day, an intense effect on viewers. Efforts to credit with Paeonius with other known late 5th century originals or copies have been unsuccessful.

The Nike of Paeonius, Museum of Olympia Opposite Page: Reproduction of the Nike of Paeonius (plaster cast) 5th cent BC.

PRAXITELES

Early 4th- 330 BC

One of the most important sculptors of Ancient Greece.
His great virtuosity and his affair with the courtesan Phryne
seem to have determined his artistic destiny. Even though
it is estimated that Praxiteles created about seventy statues
-among these many dedicated to Aphrodite the goddess of beauty-
only the Hermes with the Infant Dionysus in Olympia,
the engraved plaques of the statues of the Apollonian Triad,
and the bronze statue of a youth found in the sea off Marathon
can be attributed to him with certainty.

His life

Praxiteles lived in Athens, possibly also his birthplace, during the 4th century. BC. His father was the sculptor Ciphisodotus and he had two sons, Ciphisodotus and Timarchus, who were also sculptors.

Pausanias mentioned that Praxiteles' art reached its pinnacle during 340 BC. It was also to this period, around the middle of the 4th century, that his relationship with the courtesan Phryne, his frequent model, must date. His relationship with Phryne and his journey to Asia Minor must have been landmark events in the life of Praxiteles because they are immediately and decisively associated with his artistic creativity. It is possible that Phryne was the model for the statues of Aphrodite.

His work

Even though Praxiteles is better known for his marble sculptures, he worked with equal facility in bronze. His father taught him the art of sculpting marble and casting bronze. He collaborated with the painter Niceas to add color to his statues (since all statues were painted).

Ancient sources attribute a large number of works to Praxiteles, around seventy. Few of them have been identified with any degree of certainty. The Hermes with the Infant Dionysus in Olympia, discovered during excavations of the site in 1877, is considered an original piece, as well as the engraved plaques of the statues of the Apollonian Triad, and the bronze statue of a youth found in the sea off Marathon.

All of his other works exist only in copies and have been attributed to him mainly based on the characteristics of his technique. Some of Praxiteles' work depicted nymphs, maeniads and caryatids, while other pieces were allegorical. Most of his work, however, consisted of statues of the gods. His most important works were, among others, the group of statues of Apollo, Artemis and Leto in Mantinea in the Peloponnese, Apollo and Artemis, Apollo Sauroktonos (Lizard-Killer), the Aphrodite of Cnidos in Asia Minor, the Resting Satyr, the Eros in Thespies, which Praxiteles had given to the famous courtesan of antiquity and his lover Phryne, and other works.

Because Praxiteles' work took him to many cities in Greece and Asia Minor, samples of his art were found scattered all over the Hellenic world and were the object of such admiration on the part of his contemporaries that at times it became absurd. The ancient writers stressed his great virtuosity and considered him the equal to Phidias and Polyclitus. They also admired the way he portrayed human and especially female beauty- hence the many depictions of Aphrodite.

His aesthetic ideal was a youthful beauty, far removed from any violent emotion. He was more interested in the difficulties each individual figure presented rather than in large compositions. Liberated from the majestic and imposing tradition of Phidias' art and Polyclitus' chiastic arrangement of form, Praxiteles introduces to Greek sculpture the depiction of gods with slight bodies, presents Aphrodite fully nude for the first time, and portrays Eros and the Satyrs as handsome, melancholy, and dreamy youths. The facial expressions of Praxiteles' figures are almost unique in Greek sculpture for the tenderness, sweetness and serenity that characterize them. The classical stance of the athletic body has now been replaced by the much more natural attitude of a body that is portrayed as leaning indolently against a support, usually a tree trunk, bent sharply at the waist so that the body's vertical axis creates a perfect *sigma (Σ)*.

Thus Praxiteles became the creator of a refined artistic style, which succeeded in expressing not only the perfection of the human body but also the feeling and soul of the person portrayed. Praxiteles' influence on his successors was immense.

Right Page: The Hermes of Praxiteles, ca 330 BC, Museum of Olympia.

Below: The Cnidian Aphrodite, ca 350 BC, Louvre Museum, Paris.

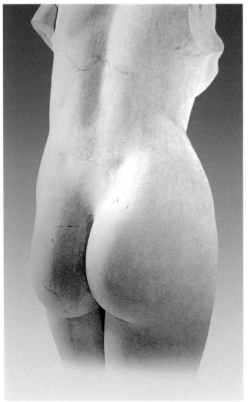
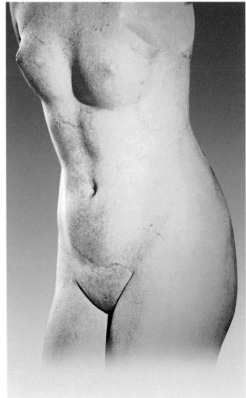

SCOPAS

ca 395 – last quarter 4th cent. BC

His life and work

His family came from the island of Paros. His father
was the Parian sculptor Aristandrus who, it seems,
exerted a special influence on his son's creative pursuits.
We have little information on his life. At the start of his
career he must have studied sculpture at his father's
side. Based on accounts that came down to us concerning his creative output as, as well as the locations
where he was active it appears that Scopas lived and
worked in the Peloponnese and in Asia Minor.

He appears to have had a restless artistic
temperament, when compared to Praxiteles and
other sculptors of his era, who remained devoted to
sculpture; Scopas and his circle expanded their artistic horizons; he turned his talents to
architecture as well. He dared to express passion and ardor through his work in a period
when Athens looked back to her classical greatness, evidencing absolutely no desire to
identify with the explosive temperament of the Parian artist.

Scopas' main interest was sculpting in marble. From recorded eyewitness accounts of
the period—the sole descriptions of his works—we know that among his great works of
art were:

- The statue of Athena Pronaos in the temple of Apollo Ismian in Thebes. The cult statue
of Artemis Eucleia is mentioned as being by Scopas.
- The statues of Aphrodite, Pothos (Longing) and Himeros (Desire) located in the temple
of Samothrace.
- The statues of Leto and Ortygia at Ephesus.
- The statues of Athena and Dionysus at Cnidos.
- The grouping of Asclepius and Hygeia at Gortys in Arcadia.
- A cult statue for the worship of Hecate at Argos.
- The statue of Heracles in the Sikyon Gymansium.

Experts speculate that Scopas' Maenad, a piece that according to written testimony
evoked matchless sensations, had also been placed in another temple of Sikyon.

However, the benchmark of Scopas' art is the temple of Alea Athena at Tegea in Arcadia. According to the testimony of Pausanias, the creation of this temple was assigned to
Scopas sometime after 395 BC—there is no precise date for when work began—to stand
on the site of a previous temple that had burned down. Even though the temple's architectural treatment may be termed extravagant, the plasticity of the sculpture and the general architectural decoration constitute the greatest validation of Scopas' artistic ability.

In the matter of the Mausoleum of Halicarnassus, which had been central to previous attempts to determine Scopas' technique, it has been established that the activities of Scopas and his associates were confined solely to sculpting certain statues that served to embellish the monument. In summary, the descriptions of his works and the Roman copies that have survived testify that Scopas possessed the artistic virtues of genius. His figures revolt, suffer, rejoice and are not content in the reality of an Athenian society that, having lost its classical magnificence, seemed unwilling to dream of a new future. And Scopas' work grants us the full magnificence of their expression.

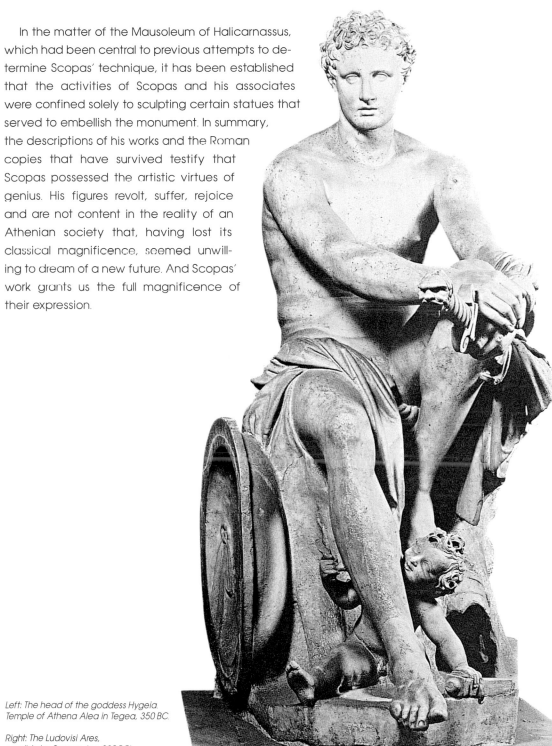

Left: The head of the goddess Hygeia.
Temple of Athena Alea in Tegea, 350 BC.

Right: The Ludovisi Ares,
possibly by Scopas (ca 330 BC).
Copy, Nazionale Romano Museum, Rome.

LYSIPPUS
390-305 BC

His life and work

Greek sculptor of the second half of the 4th century who worked in bronze, Lysippus came from the city of Sicyon in Corinthia. He was also favoured by Alexander the Great and is considered to be one of the greatest sculptors not only of antiquity but of all times.

His work belongs to the late classical art period (430–400 BC) and demonstrates all the features that distinguish art during the new era that came to be known as Hellenistic. He crafted the foundations on which the sculptors of that era would build, and is therefore rightfully considered the father of Hellenistic sculpture. Lysippus was a most prolific creator. Pliny attributes to him 1500 works scattered amongst a multitude of ancient cities.

Of his work, only certain marble copies remain. In his works Lysippus covered the entire subject matter of ancient sculpture. He depicted gods, heroes, muses, athletes, kings -primarily Alexander- generals, philosophers, poets, etc. Some of the new elements Lysippus introduced and which set him apart from earlier sculptors, especially Polyclitus, were the increase in the length of the body and the scaling down of the size of the head so that the relation from 1:7 became 1:8; and the free movement of figures in three dimensional space. The latter quality is easily perceived in the famous *Apoxyomenos* whose right arm is held forward and the left is bent before his chest, with the distance separating the two hands from the body reinforcing the illusion of three-dimensional space. For the first time in classical art this figure Lysippus created appears to be opening itself up to the viewer. Lysippus founded a vibrant school that spread his traditions to latter generations. His was the last great name in the history of Greek sculpture.

From Lysippus' numerous works, the following stand out:
- The Apoxyomenos, i.e. the athlete who is scraping oil and dust off his body after a contest.
- The colossal statue of Zeus at Tarentum that stood in the city's market place.
- Many busts and statues of Alexander the Great.
- The *Farnese Heracles* or *Resting Heracles,* a colossal statue whose powerful body was portrayed with exaggerated musculature. An exhausted Heracles leans against his

club, while his right arm rests wearily behind him at his waist, his head revealing all the hero's bodily and mental fatigue.

- The *Heracles Epitrapezios,* used to decorate the table of Alexander the Great.
- The statue of *Time* in Olympia. A novel creation, an allegorical representation of *Time,* opportunity in other words. It represented a nude running youth whose long hair waving forward signified that whoever was able could seize Time (Opportunity) before it passed by.
- The *25 Macedonian Companions* who fell at the battle of Granicus, placed at Dion in Macedonia.
- The statue of *Hellos* in his chariot on Rhodes.
- The statue of *Socrates* in the Pompeion in Keramikos in Athens, which differed in both style and expression from a previous statue erected by the Athenians shortly after his death. Contrary to that statue's seated and pensive state, Lysippus' *Socrates* was on his feet ready to debate.

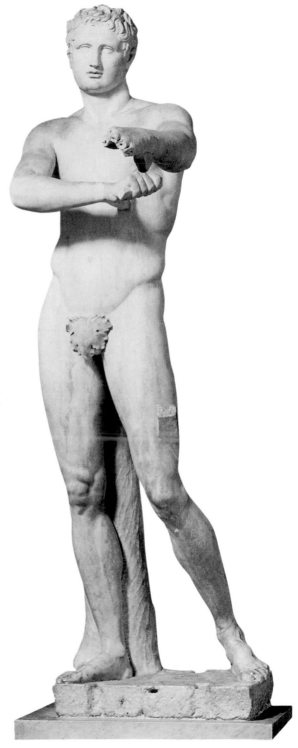

Left: Bronze Roman copy of a statue representing Hermes, attributed to Lysippus.

Right: The Apoxyomenos, ca 330 BC, Roman copy in the Vatican.

The female divinities Hestia and Dione with Aphrodite, from the east pediment of the Parthenon (British Museum, London).

III. PAINTING

ZEUXIS OR ZEUXIPPUS

2nd half of 5th century BC

His life and work

We know of Zeuxis' fame in the ancient world only from the references in texts of the period that constitute the sole source of information on his work. In these references he is styled *Heraclean* although nowhere do the texts specify which of the ancient cities (nearly ten) bearing the name Heraclea was his true birthplace.

The fame of this great painter quickly spread beyond the borders of Athens and Archelaus, King of Macedonia invited him to come to Pella to decorate his palace there.

Zeuxis must have studied with the great painter Apollodorus, to whom he owed the great progress he made in sketching his work. References to this great painter speak of him as "kalos kagathos", literally beautiful and good, in other words, an exemplary Athenian citizen.

Legend has it that when the city of Croton invited Zeuxis to portray the beauty of divine Helen, the painter wanted to see all the maidens of the city nude so as to select the most beautiful one as his model. Although Zeuxis' works were lost, their memory was nevertheless preserved by the great men of antiquity, the Sophist Lucian amongst them, whose work constitutes an admirable example of early art criticism. From the accounts, some of Zeuxis' most important works were the following:

- *Eros crowned with Flowers,* mentioned by Aristophanes in his work *Acharnians.*
- A remarkable and compelling representation of a flock of birds dallying with the fruit of a ripe vine. Remarking on this work Pliny wrote that the grapes seemed so true to life that the birds flying around them were fooled and would approach to peck at the fruit.
- *A Centaur Family,* preserved in all its glory through the writings of Lucian.

Zeuxis was exceptional because of the various techniques he invented to render his work. His famous *monochromata ex abo* (monochromes in white) technique enabled him to depict figures on a white background. The texts also reveal that he had an exceptional facility in the use and treatment of color.

He was once accused of taking a long time to complete a work. He retorted that it took him a long time to paint for a lasting period, wanting to emphasize that the creation of any work that lasts through time takes time.

POLYGNOTUS

5th century BC

His life and work

It Is held by many that painting originated with Polygnotus. He was born on the island of Thasos. His father Aglaophon was also a painter. His greatest achievements are thought to date from the second quarter of the 5th century BC. He neither lived nor worked on Thasos but traveled and stayed in many cities, amongst them Athens, Delphi, Plataea, Thespies.

Unfortunately, none of Polygnotus' works have survived. From passages in ancient texts comes the information that Polygnotus developed painting to such an extent that many describe him as the originator of this art. New forms and new shapes, pioneering methods of rendering space and depth are only some of the innovations attributed to Polygnotus' painting technique. Aristotle considered that the painter depicted character (*ethos*) because, as he noted, Polygnotus' figures portrayed individual emotions.

Aelianus [1] described his art as having "precision, passion and ethos"; Lucian [2] observed that he elaborated the garments on his figures "in great detail". Pliny [3] attributed many innovations to Polygnotus, such as that he was the first to paint female figures in transparent multicoloured clothing and the first to create figures with open mouths showing teeth, thus relieving their faces of their archaic rigidity. As regards his technique, Polygnotus probably used a light colored plaster and the colors white, black, red and yellow.

According to these texts we may conclude that his paintings were to be found in the Anaceio, temple of the Dioscuri on the northern edge of the Acropolis (he painted the wedding of the daughters of Leucippus), in the Poikili Stoa and the Theseion (*The Sack of Troy* and the *Battle of the Centaurs*), and at Plataea. His most important work is said to have been the murals of the *Sack of Troy* and *Nekuia*, executed for the Lesche (assembly hall) of the Cnidians at Delphi (the graded placement of the figures creates perspective as does the concealing of the lower parts of their bodies behind lines, showing the relief of the ground). He received no monetary reward for this work but rather was awarded the great honor of a Delphic ambassadorship. Also, in the so-called Pinacotheke of the Propylaea, he painted scenes inspired by the Homeric epics and the traditions of other mythological cycles of antiquity directly on walls or on portable tablets.

1. Claudius Aelianus: Sophist of Roman origin who wrote in Greek (170-235 AD).
2. Lucian: Sophist and author from Samosat in Syria (2nd cent. AD). See p. 196).
3. Pliny the Elder (Gaius Plinius Secundus): Roman military man and writer of a scientific encyclopedia entitled *Natural History* (23-79 AD).

LEADERS-POLITICIANS, ORATORS

The third chapter presents all those who distinguished themselves in the use of discourse. Words used in the service of politics and of the law, words used to proclaim and to advise, to rejoice and to write history.
This section contains:

▸ The most important politicians and leaders of Greek antiquity whose beliefs determined the evolution of the ancient world. They are Aristides, Themistocles, Cimon, Miltiades, Pericles and Alexander the Great.

▸ The orators Lysias, Aeschines, Demosthenes, Lycurgus and Isocrates, who with abundant eloquence regurarly addressed the popular assembly (demos).

▸ The writers Archimedes, Aesop, Arrian, Diogenes Laertius, Herodotus, Lucian, Thucydides, Xenophon, Pausanias, Plutarch and Polybius, whose works contain the most valid record of Greek history.

Pericles speaking at the Pnyx,
destroyed during the WWII (1941–1944)
bombardment of Athens.

ARISTIDES
THE JUST

540 -468 BC

Preeminent political personality
of Athens. He went down in history
as a selfless and just politician.
The leader of Athens' conservative
faction, his fervent patriotism
was acknowledged even by Themistocles,
leader of the democratic faction,
who in 482 BC exiled Aristides
to the island of Aegina.

ΤΙ ΓΑΡ ΦΙΛΤΕΡΟΝ ΑΝΔΡΙ
ΠΑΤΡΩΑΣ ΧΘΟΝΟΣ

For what does man
love more than his birthplace?

Η ΜΕΝ ΕΛΛΑΣ
ΕΝ ΜΕΣΩ ΠΑΣΗΣ ΓΗΣ,
Η Δ'ΑΤΤΙΚΗ ΤΗΣ
ΕΛΛΑΔΟΣ, ΤΗΣ ΔΕ
ΧΩΡΑΣ Η ΠΟΛΙΣ,
ΤΗΣ Δ 'ΑΥ ΠΟΛΕΩΣ
Η ΟΜΩΝΥΜΟΣ

Greece is at the center
of the world, Attica is at
the center of Greece,
Athens is at the center of Attica
and finally the Acropolis
is at the center of Athens.

ΑΡΕΤΗ ΔΕ ΚΑΝ ΘΑΝΗ
ΤΙΣ ΟΥΚ ΑΠΟΛΛΥΤΑΙ

Even after death virtue may not be lost.

His life and work

Aristides, known as the Just, was a famous Athenian politician and general. Under no circumstances would he tolerate falsehood, deception or hypocrisy. A genuine patriot and selfless politician he was an ardent supporter of the Athenian state. His father was named Lysimachus and he was born in the municipality of Alopeces, in the south of Athens. He died somewhere in the Black Sea region while traveling in the service of Athens, his homeland.

One of the ten generals who had participated in the battle of Marathon in 490 BC, he used all his authority to push through every measure necessary to ensure a victorious outcome. It is said that the Athenians placed the war prizes and prisoners of that battle in his care when the rest of the army sped to Phaleron to prevent a possible Persian attack.

When his turn came to become commander-in-chief of the army, he resigned and also persuaded the other eight generals to do the same so that the leadership duty fell to Miltiades who was the most experienced.

It is possible that this stance was a factor in his being elected archon (governor) of Athens the next year, while representing the conservative faction. He opposed Themistocles who, representing the democratic faction and believing that Athens should build a powerful navy, sought to forward his programs, mercantile and maritime in particular. Aristides believed that Athens should neither abandon agriculture nor allow the army to be weakened.

In 482 BC his opposition to these programs led to his being ostracized and exiled to Aegina. Three years later, after Themistocles had succeeded in fortifying the Athenian navy, he recalled Aristides from exile.

This occurred a short while before the naval battle of Salamis, either because Themistocles sensed that he would need Aristides' assistance against the new Persian danger or because he feared that Aristides desiring revenge would side with the Persians; the latter was of course impossible.

Aristides, on the contrary, showed a great deal of forbearance as well as great patriotism. Not only did he participate in the naval battle of Salamis but he also agreed to fight under Themistocles.

He also distinguished himself during the battle at Plataea in 479 BC, and in 478 BC, at the head of the Greek fleet, he sailed to Cyprus and Byzantium.

Such was the prestige that Aristides had acquired, and so honorable was his character that when the Greek allies founded the Delian League in the spring of 477 BC, they trusted his judgment so much that he was assigned the task of calculating the amount of each city-state's annual contribution to the League's treasury. And he did this in so just a fashion that his decisions were applied without any complaint.

Rarely in history has anyone possessed such irreproachable morality, honesty, and directness. The Athenians, honoring this man's virtue, buried him at public expense, provided dowries for his daughters and gave a generous gift to his son.

One of the ablest politicians
of ancient Greece, he was
a member of the democratic faction
and one of the most capable
generals in the whole
of Greece. Thanks to his genius,
his good judgment and his ability
to make the best use of whatever
happened, he was able to secure
many important victories against
the Persians as well as to contribute
significantly to
the establishment of Athens
as the major maritime and
mercantile power of Greece.

THEMISTOCLES
525 -459 BC

ΑΚΟΥΣΟΝ ΜΕΝ ΠΑΤΑΞΟΝ ΔΕ
Strike, if you will; but first listen.

His life and work

Themistocles was a charismatic politician, a member of the democratic faction of Athens as well as one on the ablest generals throughout the whole of Greece. He was active during the first half of the 5th century. Born in Athens he died in Magnesia in Asia Minor. He was the son of Neocles, a scion of the house of Lycomedes, his mother Abrotonos came from either Caria or Thrace.

Most of the information we have on his childhood and early years comes from Plutarch. Thus we learn that Themistocles was brash and curious, daring and ambitious, contradictory and abstruse and often led by his innate impetuousness. Themistocles himself is said to have commented on this subject that unruly colts, when properly trained, made the best horses.

In contrast to Plutarch, Thucydides considered him an admirable man. He praises Themistocles's instinctive good sense, his capacity for swift thought, his ability to make the best of current events and to foresee future ones, his good judgement, his insightfulness and his natural genius. His innate political gifts resulted in his becoming a member of a faction that aimed at eliminating Persia, the great threat to Greece. The victory achieved by Miltiades at Marathon caused his ambition to grow and he was known to repeat that the triumph of Miltiades would not allow him to sleep.

After the death of Miltiades, Themistocles entered the political arena unobstructed and began instituting his plans to make Athens the most powerful and glorious of cities. He persuaded the Athenians to move their naval base of operations from Phaleron to the better natural harbor of Piraeus, and to place the profits from the mines in the service of constructing warships. Being both observant and insightful he was the first to understand that only with naval backing would Athens be able to face the coming conflict with the Persians. As a result, within a short period of time Athens had 200 triremes. It was mainly thanks to Themistocles that the Greek cities met in council in Corinth during the summer of 480 BC, whereupon the decision was taken to form an alliance to reject jointly the demands for surrender issued by King Xerxes of Persia in 481 BC.

These events were followed by the battle at Thermopylae and the deployment of the fleet at Artemision. After the Persians advanced against Athens and its inhabitants fled the city, the contest moved to the sea. In 480 BC on September 20, the naval battle took place in the narrow straits of Salamis, according to Themistocles' plan, which proved to be a stroke of genius. Themistocles was the acknowledged savior of Greece and was awarded the second battle prize as the first went to the Spartan admiral Eurybiades, who had been assigned the overall command by Themistocles himself. The rebuilding of Athens began in 478 BC, again at Themistocles' instigation and on his initiative. New walls were constructed around Athens, and Piraeus was fortified. These measures laid the foundations for Athens to become the major maritime and mercantile power of Greece.

But in 470 BC, his opponents in the conservative party, the party of Aristides and Cimon, succeeded in having him ostracized. He then fled to Argos, and from Argos to Corfu (Kerkyra), and from there to the court of Admetus, King of the Molossi in Epirus. Since his opponents continued to persecute him, Admetus sent him to Pydna in Macedonia from whence he traveled via Ephesus to Persia, where King Artaxerxes greeted him with great honors and ceded the revenues of three cities in Asia Minor to provide him with a living.

Artaxerxes of course, was not doing this out of sheer altruism. In 461 BC he asked Themistocles to lead the Persian navy against that of his homeland. Themistocles found himself in a tragically difficult position and chose to die.

His remains were later transferred in secret to Attica and buried at the entrance of the port of Piraeus. His descendants were awarded honors that continued to the days of Plutarch.

MILTIADES
550-489 BC

Renowned Greek general and politician
whose name is mostly associated with
the successful outcome of the battle
at Marathon in 490 BC against the
Persians. It was this battle as well as
a previous successful campaign
against the island of Lemnos
that saved Miltiades from later
being condemned to death after
a political failure on Paros.
Although he died in prison,
the Athenians always honored him
and acknowledged his greatness
as a politician.

His life and work

A renowned Greek general and politician, Miltiades wed Hegesipyle, daughter of a Thracian prince, with whom he had two children, Cimon and Elpinike. He was responsible for the victory at the famous battle of Marathon in 490 BC. Historians maintain that the victory at Marathon saved not only Athens but also the whole of Greece from the Persian yoke. And a central factor in this victory was Miltiades' bravery, battlefield experience and decisiveness.

He was an ingenious and experienced general who, instead of conforming to the standard battle strategy, introduced and applied a new one, and the innovations he employed on the field of battle were mainly responsible for the Greek victory.

Case in point: Once the Persians had disembarked at Marathon the question was whether Athens should wait for the enemy to reach Athens and engage them at the city walls or whether the battle should take place on the plain of Marathon.

Miltiades strongly supported the second solution because first, the walls of Athens were not very strong; second, Athens had few archers -which were absolutely necessary to defend fortress walls successfully- while on the contrary the enemy had many; and third, the enemy forces would destroy the surrounding countryside, an outcome that would have a negative effect on the Athenian army's morale.

On the contrary, the plain of Marathon, with the sea on one side and a line of hills on the other had only two narrow means of access that could be relatively easily controlled by the Athenian forces. Additionally, the hills would provide the Greeks with a good base facilitating both attack and re-supply. And lastly, the narrow access passages would negate the great numerical advantage the Persians possessed.

Miltiades' above proposal proved very ingenious and the strategy he applied, namely to lighten the center and reinforce the flanks of the Athenian formation was later imitated by great generals throughout history.

Miltiades, the main architect of the victory against the Persians, belonged to a series of great men, who, expressing the temper of that age, laid the foundations for the greatness of Athens, and after the Persian defeat swiftly placed Athens at the forefront. Legend has it thathis family, the Philaids, was descended from the heroes Aeacus and Ajax. In 518 he succeeded his brother Stisagorus as ruler of the peninsula of Thrace. In 515 BC, at the head of a mercenary troupe he put down an insurrection in Thrace and two years later followed Darius I, King of Persia in his campaign against the Scythians.

In 498 BC Persia invaded Thrace causing Miltiades to relocate to Athens with many followers and treasures.

In 489 BC, Athens sent Miltiades to liberate the Cyclades Isles from the Persians. He was unsuccessful and he himself was wounded.

He was then accused by Xanthippus of having campaigned for personal reasons against the island of Paros, fell out of favor and was sentenced to pay a fine of 50 talents During this campaign Athens had entrusted Miltiades with a fleet of 70 warships and he had promised to bring back much gold. Miltiades sought to punish Paros because the island had allied itself with the Persians and, as punishment for this treason, to extract a fine of 100 talents. The campaign was unsuccessful and Miltiades came back to face a tide of popular outrage.

It is obvious that the Athenians took a very strict stance towards their rulers. Or rather, as Herodotus noted, they kept them under tight supervision and did not hesitate to punish them when they thought it necessary. Miltiades was thankfully saved from being condemned to death for his failure against Paros by the victory at Marathon and a previous successful campaign against the island of Lemnos. Nevertheless as he was unable to pay the fine imposed, was imprisoned and died a short while later, as a result of the bad conditions that prevailed in the prison as well as the wounds he suffered during the siege of Paros.

In the matter of the fine, the tale is that a rich family friend later paid it, thus permitting Miltiades' son Cimon to assume his rights as an Athenian citizen, of which he had been deprived due to the unpaid fine. Miltiades' tragic end did not, however, affect the respect and recognition accorded his historic role, because his fellow citizens never forgot that it was to him they owed their victory over Persia.

Miltiades was also honored by Athens for his contribution to the victory at Marathon. It is said that on a site close to the tomb they erected a monument to him, and this may have been what destroyed Themistocles' peace of mind (see page 149).

CIMON SON OF MILTIADES

506 – 449 BC

The son of Miltiades, Cimon played a significant role in Athenian politics. His political virtues were first noted by Aristides the Just in 480 BC, during the naval battle of Salamis that ended with the celebrated victory of the Greeks over the Persians. He rose to the rank of general in 478 BC and his name was subsequently linked to a series of splendid military achievements.

His life and work

Athenian politician and general, the son of Hegesipyle, daughter of the king of Thrace and of Miltiades. From his mother he is said to have inherited many pleasant traits of demeanor as well as of character. His father, a politician and general, was the architect of the Athenian victory against Persia at Marathon. He was first elected general in 476 BC and continued being re-elected until 462 BC.

Cimon was tall with thick curly hair and a handsome face. Orphaned from a young age, he had not received a good education, but he could ride, play the lyre and was interested in poetry. He was likable and generous.

A man of military talents, but with a harsh and tempestuous character, a man who could not easily be mastered, Cimon was the type of individual who sought out and built power. During his youth his life had been full, restless and replete with amusements, and he seemed a sensual but strong-willed man capable of restraining his passions. When, after the ill-fated expedition against Paros, his father was condemned to pay a heavy fine of 50 talents, Cimon paid the sum, as his father was unable to do so. Yet another version of the story had a rich friend of the family paying the fine. Cimon was thus able to re-acquire the rights he had been deprived of due to the unpaid fine. Cimon first made his presence known on the political stage of Athens on the eve of the naval battle of Salamis when he ascended the Acropolis and dedicated the reigns of his horse to Athena.

Then, although a political foe of Themistocles who led the Greek navy at Salamis, he was the first to board a ship along with his followers and distinguished himself for his valor during the naval battle, which concluded with the celebrated victory of the Greeks against the Persians in September of 480 BC. His reputation grew to such an extent that upon Aristides' death, he succeeded him at the head of the conservative faction.

It is true that the first person to perceive Cimon's abilities was Aristides the Just who took the opportunity to introduce him into the political arena as a member of the aris- tocratic faction. This occurred a short while after 480 BC. Cimon acquired the rank of general in 478 BC, and from 476 BC until 463 BC, he led the forces of the Delian League. In 475 BC, he conquered the isle of Scyros, casting out the pirates, and returned triumphant to Athens bringing with him what were believed to be the bones of the Athenian hero Theseus, said to have been buried on that island.

He proved to be a great military leader, and expanded the Athenian confederacy with the annexation of Eiona, a Thracian city that contained a large Persian garrison, and of Scyros, from whence he cast out the terrible Dolopian pirates who had been harassing the Athenian traders. Later he also conquered Carystos and Naxos in 469 BC.

But Cimon's greatest military achievement was in 466 BC against the Persian fleet at the estuary of the Eurymedon River, where the Persians had gathered a naval and land force. Cimon mounted a surprise attack against the Persians and scattered them, suc- ceeding in either capturing or destroying 200 of the 350 mostly Phoenician ships that were assembled at the mouth of the river.

This victory of Cimon against the barbarians renewed the impressive impact of the Greek accomplishment in Mycale where the Persian fleet was torched by the Greeks Leotychides and Xanthippus in 479 BC.However, like all great leaders -Themistocles and Aristides, Pericles, Nicias, Alcibiades, Phocion, and Demosthenes- Cimon did not escape popular rancor. Accusations of suspect and anti-democratic behavior were responsible for his being exiled for five years to Boeotia, until he was summoned back by Pericles, who, even though he was his political opponent, recognised his value and honest patriotism.

In 449 BC Cimon grew ill and died after defeating the Persians off Cyprus at the head of a 200-ship fleet. On its way back to Athens the Hellenic fleet encountered the fleet of the Phoenician and Cilician allies of Persia. Upon seeing the Athenian fleet, and unaware that Cimon had died, their leaders grew afraid and were routed. As Plutarch pointed out, Cimon was victorious even after his death.

He was buried with great honors in Athens and will always be an example of straight- forward patriotism, pure character, shrewd purposefulness and strategic genius.

PERICLES

495 - 429 BC

Major political personality identified
with the apogee of classical Athens.
The years during which he governed
Athens were dubbed the Golden Age
because Pericles introduced democratic
concepts, contributed to the flourishing
of the arts and endowed Athens
with the most magnificent monuments
of art and civilization. He was unable
to avert the Peloponnesian War; he lost
both his sons in that conflict, which also
led later to his being deprived of his
position as general and fined. A short
while before his death the Athenian
republic once again entrusted
the government of the city to him.

ΤΟ ΕΥΔΑΙΜΟΝ ΤΟ
ΕΛΕΥΘΕΡΟΝ,
ΤΟ Δ'ΕΛΕΥΘΕΡΟΝ ΤΟ
ΕΥΨΥΧΟΝ ΚΡΙΝΑΝΤΕΣ
ΜΗ ΠΕΡΙΟΡΑΣΘΕ ΤΟΥΣ
ΠΟΛΕΜΙΚΟΥΣ ΚΙΝΔΥΝΟΥΣ

Knowing that happiness
means freedom and freedom
means valour, you must not cower
before the dangers of war.

ΕΓΩ ΓΑΡ ΗΓΟΥΜΑΙ ΠΟΛΙΝ
ΠΛΕΙΟ ΞΥΜΠΑΣΑΝ
ΟΡΘΟΥΜΕΝΗΝ ΩΦΕΛΕΙΝ
ΤΟΥΣ ΙΔΙΩΤΑΣ Η
ΚΑΘ'ΕΚΑΣΤΟΝ ΤΩΝ ΠΟΛΙΤΩΝ
ΕΥΠΡΑΓΟΥΣΑΝ ΑΥΘΡΟΑΝ ΔΕ
ΣΦΑΛΛΟΜΕΝΗΝ

I believe that if a city
as a whole is prosperous,
it serves its citizens much better
than when each citizen separately
is happy, but the city as a whole
is miserable.

ΦΙΛΟΚΑΛΟΥΜΕΝ ΓΑΡ
ΜΕΤ' ΕΥΤΕΛΕΙΑΣ ΚΑΙ
ΦΙΛΟΣΟΦΟΥΜΕΝ
ΑΝΕΥ ΜΑΛΑΚΙΑΣ

We are lovers of
beauty without extravagance
and lovers of wisdom
without effeminacy.

ΑΝΔΡΩΝ ΕΠΙΦΑΝΩΝ ΠΑΣΑ ΓΗ ΤΑΦΟΣ

For famous men have the whole earth as their memorial.

His life

The greatest politician of ancient Greece and leader of Athens for over thirty years, Pericles ruled Athens during the city's classical period.

His father was Xanthippus, the general who had defeated the Persians at Mycale in 479 BC, while his mother Agariste was the niece of Cleisthenes the founder of the Athenian democracy. Legend has it that a few days after dreaming she had given birth to a lion, Agariste gave birth to Pericles, whose long head was disproportionately large compared to the rest of his body. This may explain why artists usually portrayed Pericles wearing a helmet in order to avoid displeasing him by revealing this physical defect.

His wealthy and aristocratic family made certain he received an exceptional education. His instructors were the philosophers Zeno of Elea and Anaxagoras of Clazomenae; the influence of the latter on Pericles' intellectual and moral development must have been great. Pericles, in turn, was one of the first politicians of antiquity to recognize that politicians also benefit from a pilosophical education.

His artistic education was shaped by the great musical theoreticians, Damon and Pythocleides.

It was therefore impossible for Pericles to be anything other than a well-rounded personality. Undoubtedly, early associations with all the brilliant personages of Athens also contributed to his emergence as a political genius.

His work

In 463 BC at the age of 27, he first involved himself in politics, sponsored by the democratic faction. He became the faction's deputy leader and later took control after the murder of the party's leader Ephialtes. He kept this office until his death; for 14 consecutive years the deme of Athens elected him to the office of general.

Pericles, as the *de facto* regulator of the political life of Athens, the general and governor of the city, sought to advance and strengthen democratic government, increase the military strength of Athens, consolidate the hold of Athens throughout Greece and develop a multifaceted cultural project which would consist of promoting arts and letters, developing great civic and public works and decorating the city with works of art.

It is to Pericles that Athens owed its evolution into the political and cultural center of Greece. Therefore this era is rightfully known as the Age of Pericles or the Golden Age of Pericles. Following is a brief outline of Pericles' achievements in this regard.

Among Pericles' peaceful pursuits was the establishment of the Athenian hegemony by founding colonies and installing Athenian citizens as land claimants in critical locations, thus ensuring not only that an out-of-work populace was employed but also that Athenian political influence existed in pivotal geographic areas. Among the great colonies then founded were: Thurii in southern Italy, where many great intellectuals moved including the Sophist philosopher Protagoras and the historian Herodotus, and Amphipolis, near the estuary of the river Strymon which ensured Athenian influence over Thrace and the power to exploit the area's rich minerals and timber.

Pericles also installed Athenian colonists in Amisus and Astacus in the Sea of Marmara thus acquiring control over the Bosphorus and the Dardanelles. He also sent colonists to the islands of Euboea, Andros and Naxos.

Thanks to these tactics Athenian economic and political influence was extended over a great portion of the western as well as the eastern Mediterranean. The economy of Athens flourished and abundant wealth flowed into the city. This wealth was used by Pericles to realise the second part of his political program: the creation of public works and the embellishment of the city with timeless works of art.

Pride of place was granted to the works on the Acropolis. The artistic supervision was assigned to the great sculptor Phidias. The architects Ictinus and Callicrates created the designs for the construction of the timeless masterpiece that was to be the Parthenon, while Phidias created the gold and ivory statue of Athena Parthenos that stood within it.

The Propylaea was erected according to a plan by Mnesicles. A conservatory where musical competitions took place was also constructed, as well as the Theseion, a temple dedicated to the god Hephaestus.

Handsome Doric temples were built at Cape Sounion and Ramnous, while Ictinus designed the Telesterio erected in Eleusis. Finally great projects turned Piraeus into a beautiful city as well as the largest port in the Mediterranean.

Pericles was memorable for his superior character, his earnest thought and high-minded speech, devoid of any obscenity or vulgarity, as well as his sober mien, calm carriage and modest dress. He always spoke in a low tone of voice, never allowing passion to overcome him.

He associated himself with the democratic faction, as he preferred to support the interests of the poor multitudes rather than the rich few.

The high level of his intellect and the perfectionism he exhibited in the execution of his projects, which according to Plato added to his natural genius, were gained from natural science from which he took all that was suitable for the art of speeches. Thus he proved himself greater than all the others. So much so, that he was dubbed Olympian, possibly because he was considered equal to the Olympian gods, possibly because of the splendid monuments with which he adorned Athens, or possibly because of his political and military superiority.

TIMELINE FROM THE "GOLDEN AGE" OF PERICLES
TO THE EARLY 4th BC CENTURY

450 BC: The construction of the great projects begins in Athens under the aegis of Pericles. These are the Propylaea, the Parthenon and the Temple of Nike Apteros. Artistic supervision is assigned to the sculptor Phidias. The architects Ictinus and Callicrates and Nesicles, the sculptors Alcamenes and Agoracritus, and the painter Polygnotus are also employed on the Acropolis projects.

447 BC: Death of the Theban lyric poet Pindar.

446 BC: The historian Herodotus reads his Histories in public in Athens and the city rewards him with ten talents.

441/0 BC: Birth of the orator Lysias, an Athenian metic; The Samian war begins.

438 BC: The foundations of the new Parthenon, dedicated to Athena Parthenos, are laid on the Acropolis.

436 BC: Birth of the orator Isocrates.

431 BC: Start of the Peloponnesian War. The Spartan king Archidamus invades Attica.

430 BC: A great plague spreads in Athens.
Birth of the historian Xenophon.

429 BC: Death of Pericles.

428 BC: Mytilene secedes from the Delian League.
Death of the philosopher Anaxagoras.

427 BC: The sophist Gorgias arrives as an ambassador in Athens.

425 BC: Lesbos secedes from the Delian League. The Spartans lay siege to Pylos. Athens receives a peace proposal that is rejected at the instigation of Cleon.

424 BC: Athens is defeated at Delion. Socrates participates as a hoplite (infantryman) in this battle. The Spartan king Brasidas captures Amphipolis. Thucydides, who in his capacity as general was unable to defend the city, is exiled.
Death of the historian Herodotus.

422 BC: The Spartan king Brasidas and the Athenian politician Cleon are killed at Amphipolis.

421 BC: Signing of the Peace of Nicias.
Construction begins on the Erechthion on the Acropolis in Athens.

420 BC: Alcibiades is elected general for the first time.

418 BC: The Spartans defeat the Peloponnesian allies of Athens at the battle of Mantineia.

415 BC: Melos is destroyed by the Athenian army.
A large Athenian fleet commanded by Alcibiades, Lamachus and Nicias sets off for Sicily.
The scandal over the mutilation of the Herms erupts. Alcibiades is summoned to Athens to explain himself but escapes and seeks asylum in Sparta.
Protagoras is tried in Athens on charges of impiety.

414 BC: Athens lays siege to Syracuse.

413 BC: Total destruction of the Athenians at Syracuse.

411 BC: The first oligarchic coup takes place in Athens and the Council of 400 is set up. Alcibiades is recalled. Under the command of generals Thrasybulus and Thrasyllus the Athenian army on Samos remains true to the ideals of democracy.

410 BC: Alcibiades is victorious at Cyzicus. Sparta sues for peace but guided by Cleophon, the popular assembly of Athens rejects the offer.
Restoration of democracy in Athens.
Death of the sophist Protagoras.

409 BC: Work on the Erechthion begins again.

408 BC: Alcibiades is once again elected general.

407 BC: After the Athenian fleet is defeated at Notion, Alcibiades is forced to flee.
Victory of Athens at the naval battle of Arginousai. The Athenian generals who did not gather the bodies are tried and condemned.

405 BC: Utter defeat of Athens at the battle of Aegospotamoi. Sparta is the victor in the Peloponnesian War.

404 BC: Second oligarchic coup in Athens. The Rule of the Thirty Tyrants is established.

403 BC: Under the leadership of Thrasybulus the exiled democratic faction regains control of Athens and restores democracy.

399 BC: Socrates is condemned for corrupting the youth of Athens

396 BC: Agesilaos, King of Sparta begins preparations for a Panhellenic campaign against the Persians.

395 BC: Start of the Corinthian War.
Death of Thucydides.

394 BC: The Athenian general Conon defeats the Spartan navy at Cnidus.

390 BC: The Athenian general Iphicrates defeats the Spartans in the vicinity of Corinth.

388 BC: Plato returns to Athens and founds his Academy.

387 BC: Representatives of the Greek states travel to Sardis and sign the King's Peace imposed by the King of Persia.

384 BC: Sparta forces the citizens of Mantineia to destroy their city and then disperse. The Spartan General Phoebidas captures the Cadmea, citadel of Thebes.
Birth of Aristotle and Demosthenes.

ALEXANDER THE GREAT

356-323 BC

The great king of Macedonia and perhaps the greatest military commander that ever lived. After planning and achieving the conquest of Greece, he turned his attention to realising a much more ambitious plan: to conquer the world. Following his successful campaign over almost the whole of the known world (Asia Minor, Persia, Egypt, etc.), he set forth on the conquest of India and reached the Hydaspis River. His death and the political infighting of his successors were the two basic factors that prevented his plan from being carried out. However, Alexander succeeded in subjugating a large portion of the then known world and unifying it in one vast empire.

His life

Alexander was the son of Philip II and Olympias, daughter of the king of the Molossi of Epirus. He was born in the city of Pella in Macedonia and died in Babylon. He succeeded his father Philip II to the throne in 336 BC and was perhaps the most successful army commander of all times, as well as the most important political figure of his era. At the head of the military forces of the allied Greek city-states, he campaigned against Persia and conquered Asia, as the Athenian orator Isocrates had frequently exhorted, and his father Philip II had planned. After his death history and legend preserved the conqueror's labors for posterity.

Plutarch wrote that his father King Philip dreamed that he had had stamped the belly of his wife Olympias with a seal in the shape of a lion. His various diviners interpreted this dream to mean that the child the Queen bore would be strong and brave. In addition, on the day Alexander was born, the temple of Artemis at Ephesus, one of the Seven Wonders of the World and a Persian national symbol, burned down. The diviners considered that the destruction of this temple was a sign that something of importance would happen in Asia.

His work

According to Plutarch, even as a youth, Alexander was serious and controlled. He was endowed with rare bodily endurance and strength and with an even rarer spirit. It was thanks to his gifts that, at just 14 years of age, he was able to tame the famous horse Bucephalus, considered extremely wild and unschooled, which later became Alexander's favourite horse and inseparable companion.

Philip showed great interest in the training and education of his heir, and, in 343 BC invited the great philosopher Aristotle, the wisest of men, to the court of Pella and entrusted him with his son's upbringing. Alexander always maintained a deep respect for his tutor, as evidenced by their correspondence. Aristotle was also responsible for Alexander's love of poetry. During the entire time he was on campaign Alexander never ceased studying the three great tragedians, Aeschylus, Sophocles and Euripides, while he always kept a copy of Homer's *Iliad* under his pillow, because in that book he had discovered Achilles, the hero whose example he wished to emulate.

Alexander's courage and military genius became clear very early on at the battle of Chaeronea in 338 BC, which sealed the Macedonian conquest of Greece. In 335 BC, a year after ascending the throne, Alexander campaigned against the neighboring Illyrian, Triballan and Getan tribes, defeating them and imposing Macedonian rule upon them.

In the same year Alexander's campaigns included a lighting strike against an anti-Macedonian uprising in Greece. Thebes, the mastermind of the revolt was razed to the ground. Alexander, however, ordered that, out of respect, the house of the poet Pindar be spared.

In the fall of 335 BC, Alexander called a council of representatives from many of the Greek city-states to Corinth. Only the Spartans refused to attend, stating that it was not customary for them to be led but to lead. In any event, the council, pronounced Alexander Emperor-General of the Greeks and the cities assumed the responsibility of providing him with troops for the great expedition into Asia.

The Asian Expedition: It had been Philip who had first conceived of attacking Persia, but it was left to Alexander to put the plan into action. The true purpose was conquest and expansion, but for reasons of ideology and propaganda, this was artfully and diplomatically disguised under the cloak of a holy mission to punish Xerxes and the Persians for the atrocities and the temple desecrations that were the result of the Persian Wars.

Though numerically weaker than the opposition, Alexander's army was the finest of that period, superbly trained and with iron discipline. At the same time the army possessed extremely talented generals and naturally, was helmed by a genius, Alexander himself.

After ensuring that his realm was quiet, and leaving his trusted general Antipater in Macedonia as his regent, Alexander, accompanied by 30,000 foot and 5,000 horse, set off to conquer the world. He immediately put into effect his ingenious strategy of first conquering all the Persian holdings on the coast of Asia Minor, thus rendering the more numerous Persian navy incapable of action.

In the spring of 334 BC, after crossing the Hellespont without encountering any real Persian opposition, Alexander visited Troy where he laid a wreath on the tomb of Achilles and where, according to legend, he complained that while Achilles had Homer to sing his praises, he Alexander had found no one.

Diodotus and Eumenes, under orders from Alexander would every day record the important details of the expedition. As this diary was unfortunately destroyed in a fire in 325 BC, precious data on Alexander's expedition to Asia has been lost. The first clash took place at the Granicus River at the end of May in 334 BC and resulted in a Persian defeat. The gates of Asia Minor were now open to Alexander. He then proceeded, sometimes encountering resistance, sometimes greeted as a liberator, to Sardis where he laid the foundations for a temple of Olympian Zeus, and then to Ephesus, Miletus, Halicarnassus, Phrygia, Caria, Lycia, Pamphilia and Pisidia.

He then reached Gordium on the Sangarius River, where legend has it he cut the famous Gordian Knot with his sword, he proceeded South to Cilicia, reached Tarsus and camped on the site of present day Alexandretta. Darius, at the head of a military force greater than Alexander's, hastened to meet him.

The two armies clashed in 333 BC at Issus, a battle that would decide the fate of Asia. Darius was defeated and fled, abandoning his family to the mercies of the Macedonian commander. As Hadrian noted in his history Alexander treated Darius' family with the respect due to royalty.

Continuing his unchecked and victorious advance, Alexander reached Phoenicia and conquered the cities of Sidon, Aradus, Biblus, Gaza, Tyre as well as the entire Phoenician fleet. He then entered Palestine and Egypt. The Egyptians who had suffered mightily under the Persian conquerors welcomed him cordially.

He visited the Libyan Desert and proceeded to the oasis of *Ammon-Zeus,* where the priests greeted him as the god's son, a title only the Egyptian kings had borne. He returned via Syria to the heart of the Persian state and met Darius' regrouped forces at Gaugamila and after crushing them conquered all the great cities: Babylon, Susa, Persepolis, and Ecbatana. With the fall of Persepolis and the death of Darius, who was murdered by Bessus the Bactrian satrap, the national war of the Greeks against the Persians was as good as ended.

Alexander had become enraptured by the vision of a global empire and sought to conquer India, despite the terrible difficulties inherent in the vast distances, the terrain and the climate. After crossing the Indus River, he advanced to the Hydaspes River where he defeated the Indian ruler Porus in one of his most brilliant victories (May–June 326 BC) and then founded two more cities Nicaea and Bucephala, the latter honoring his horse that died there.

In conclusion, he conquered part of the Indus basin and reached the river Hyphasis where his expedition ended.

The most magnificent campaign of all time had come to an end. Never before, and never again, would so many nations find themselves under one sole ruler. But Alexander was not only a great conqueror. He was also an organizer, possessed by the idea of uniting the peoples of his now vast domain. His premature death as well as the ill feeling and strife among his successors did not permit his desire for one global state where victors and vanquished would come together to be realized. Yet even though Alexander died young his achievement was timeless. Because, through his conquests, Greek civilization spread far beyond its previous borders. Asia was Hellenized, Greece itself was influenced by Eastern thought and the culmination was the birth of the civilization of the Hellenistic Age.

Although this vision of world domination was never achieved on a concrete political level, it was experienced on a cultural one. For many centuries later, an individual's identity would not be expressed so much in national terms, but rather by the fact that he dwelled in a society whose foundation was the Greek language and whose intellectual and cultural choices were influenced to a greater or lesser extent by Hellenic cultural tradition

OIMAI ΔΥΝΑΣΘΑΙ
ΤΑ ΤΟΥ ΣΩΜΑΤΟΣ
ΔΥΣΤΥΧΗΜΑΤΑ ΤΟΙΣ ΤΗΣ
ΨΥΧΗΣ ΕΠΙΤΗΔΕΥΜΑΣΙΝ
ΙΑΣΘΑΙ ΙΚΑΝΩΣ

I think physical misfortunes
can be cured satisfactorily
by mental virtues.

ΤΙΣ ΓΑΡ ΕΣΤΙΝ ΕΛΠΙΣ
ΤΟΥΣ ΑΛΛΟΥΣ
ΕΘΕΛΗΣΕΙΝ ΟΙΕΙΝ ΤΑ
ΥΠΟ ΤΩΝ ΣΤΡΑΤΗΓΩΝ
ΠΡΟΣΤΑΤΤΟΜΕΝΑ ΟΤΑΝ
ΑΥΤΟΙ ΟΥΤΟΙ ΤΟΥΣ
ΑΚΟΣΜΟΥΝΤΑΣ ΣΩΖΕΙΝ
ΠΕΙΡΩΝΤΑΙ

For what hope can we have that
the others will comply with
the orders issued by the generals,
when these lend their authority
to the attempt to save
the insubordinate?

LYSIAS

445-380 BC

Athenian orator and speechwriter.
Most of his speeches dealt with
personal issues and were mostly
forensic, written to be declaimed
before a jury. Because of the
simplicity and naturalness of the prose
Lysias used to fashion his speeches
-ensuring that he expressed to
the best of his ability the individual
voice of his clients- legal rhetoric
developed into the art of prose.

ΟΤΙ ΟΥ ΠΕΡΙ ΠΟΛΙΤΕΙΑΣ
ΕΙΣΙΝ ΑΙ ΠΡΟΣ
ΑΛΛΗΛΟΥΣ ΔΙΑΦΟΡΑΙ,
ΑΛΛΑ ΠΕΡΙ ΤΩΝ ΙΔΙΑ
ΣΥΜΦΕΡΟΝΤΩΝ ΕΚΑΣΤΩ

People's views differ not with
regard to the political system,
but to their own
personal interests.

His life

An ancient Greek orator and speechwriter who was born and died in Athens, Lysias was the son of Cephalus, a rich Syracusan weapons maker. Upon the death of his father he moved to Thurii, an Athenian colony on in Lower Italy where he was taught the art of rhetoric by the famous Syracusan orator Teisias. The tragic failure of the Athenians' Sicilian expedition forced him to return to Athens. In 404 BC, when the Thirty Tyrants seized power Lysias and his family were persecuted because of their democratic leanings. Their fortune was confiscated, his brother Polemarchus was killed and Lysias too was persecuted and forced to seek refuge in Megara. From there he assisted Thrasybulus to cast out the tyrants and when democracy was restored he returned to Athens.

Despite the assistance of his friends he was unable to gain the rights of an Athenian citizen and he dwelled in Athens having been granted certain privileges (*isoteleia*) as a metic or resident alien of Athens.

His work

Based on our information, Lysias composed approximately 425 speeches; of that number 233 are considered genuinely his. Thirty-four have come down to us, not all of them complete. There are a few of his speeches that were epideictic or showpiece works (composed for celebrations and festivals), some were political or deliberative (for the city assembly and the parliament) while most were forensic or judicial, i.e. composed to be declaimed in court by private citizens who were obliged to defend their cases on their own.

As regards the first set of speeches, their authenticity is suspect and the quality only fair. These are the *Funeral Oration* the *Olympic Oration* and, with major reservations, the *Speech on Eros*, mentioned by Plato in *Phaedrus*, and attributed by him to Lysias. The style of the *Funeral* and *Olympic orations* was strongly influenced by sophistry and does not resemble that of Lysias' forensic speeches.

The *Funeral Oration* is one of many tributes composed to the dead and to Athens that have been preserved. It is of greater value as a testimony to the evolution of ideas than as a work of literature. It was written a short while after 393 BC. It is a showpiece work and speaks of those who fell during the Corinthian War. In the celebratory *Olympic Oration* Lysias addresses himself to all the Greeks who have gathered for the Olympic Games and calls upon them to cease their civil strife and unite, principally against the tyrant of Syracuse, Dionysius. It had immediate results. The crowd plundered the magnificent stage of the attending Syracusans.

As previously mentioned, an extensive excerpt from an oration on Eros exists in Plato's *Phaedrus*. In this, Lysias compares the individual who is in love with the one who is not.

As regards his forensic speeches, the oration *Against Eratosthenes* is the only one Lysias wrote for himself and the only one that he himself delivered. It was written in 403 BC, in which the writer accuses the murderer of his brother and petitions for justice.

In the *Defense On the Murder of Eratosthenes,* Euphiletus, an average Athenian citizen, explains why he killed his wife's lover Eratosthenes -not to be confused with the tyrant Eratosthenes- and vividly unfolds his family drama before the eyes of the judges.

In the *Defense Against Simon the central topic is the rivalry and the quarrels between two Athenians for the love of Theodotus, a youth from Plataea.*

His masterpiece is the speech *On the Refusal of a Pension,* in which a poor man who is unable to work has come before the assembly and using guile and humor battles to retain his paltry pension of an obol a day.

The speech *Against Agoratus* accuses Agoratus of being a shameless slave who plotted with the oligarchs and caused the death of democratic citizens.

The speeches *Against Philon, On the Scrutiny of Evandros, For Mantitheus,* and the *Defense against a Charge of Subverting the Democracy* are also political in content.

The speeches *Against Epicratus* and *Against Nicomachus* speak of the obligations of the archons after relinquishing power.

In *Against Hyppothersus,* Lysias attempts, many years after the restoration of democracy, to regain his lost family fortune. The speech *Against the Corn Dealers* supports the interests of the wholesalers and accuses certain metics of pre-purchasing corn at a higher than the legal price.

In *Against Diogeiton,* Diogeiton is accused of having defrauded his two underage and orphaned grandchildren of their fortune while they were under his guardianship. Their sister's husband appears before the court and requests a judgment in favor of the children. The speech of the children's mother before the family council, full of maternal feeling, is essentially the main argument against Diogeiton.

In the speeches *Against Ergocles* and *Against Philocratus* Lysias became an apologist of towering radicalism and dealt with the property issues of many notables in a manner totally contrary to that which he had expressed in his speech *On the Property of Aristophanes.*

With his speech *On the Olive Stump,* or *Regarding the Enclosure of a Sacred Olive,* a member of the propertied class defends himself before the High Court with dignity and indignation against the charge that he had allegedly trespassed either against a sacred olive tree or its enclosure.

It is evident that most of Lysias' speeches dealt with personal issues. Taken together they provide us with a lively illustration of Athenian life and the portrait of a city torn apart by disputes, recrimination and high-handedness.

Lysias succeeded in giving each of his speeches a tone appropriate to each individual client, entering deep into his client's psyche, an ability that causes us to marvel

AESCHINES

389-314 BC

His life and work

Aeschines was born in Athens in 389 BC of respectable but poor parents. Thus he was unable to study at the academy of Isocrates or Plato, as did the well-to-do youths of his time. Even though he was a self-taught orator, his skill was soon recognised, thanks to his eloquence, clarity and intelligence, and his fine voice. We can learn about Aeschines' political activity from his three extant speeches, since all three of them refer to cases with a public or political content. They are known by the titles *Against Timarchus, On the False Embassy* and *Against Ctesiphon*. The occasion on which Aeschines delivered his oration *Against Timarchus* was to refute the charge brought against him in 345 BC by Timarchus, behind whom was Demosthenes, the orator's political and rhetorical adversary. Timarchus argued that in 346 BC, when Aeschines was a member of the embassy sent by Athens to negotiate the peace with Philip of Macedon, Aeschines behaved in such a way as to harm the interests of Athens and even changed his stance to the benefit of Philip. The charge against Aeschines was therefore high treason, but he was acquitted owing to his powerful speech accusing Timarchus of immoral conduct

In his speech *On the False Embassy* Aeschines was able to rebuff a virtually identical charge, this time brought by Demosthenes himself. This occurred in 342 BC. Aeschines's third oration *Against Ctesiphon* was delivered in 330 BC in a trial with Demosthenes once again as adversary, although formally it was Ctesiphon who had proposed that his friend Demosthenes be awarded a golden crown. This time Aeschines was defeated and went into voluntary exile in Rhodes. His three speeches are splendid creations of rhetorical art. As an orator, Aeschines is certainly inferior to Demosthenes, and there are times when his speech sounds empty, as does that of the Sophists. But the form of his discourse is clear, brilliant and strong. He uses irony, indignation and sarcasm persistently.

ΧΑΛΕΠΟΝ ΤΟ ΜΗ ΦΙΛΗΣΑΙ
ΧΑΛΕΠΟΝ ΤΕ ΚΑΙ ΦΙΛΗΣΑΙ

It is painful both to fall in love and not to fall in love.

DEMOSTHENES

384-322 BC

**The greatest, most famous orator
in ancient Greece and a distinguished
Athenian statesman. Demosthenes
lived during the period when
the city of Athens was threatened
by the expansionist designs
of Philip II of Macedon; thus in
his famous speeches, the Philippics
and Olynthiacs, he tried to convince
the Athenians to resist Philip
and to fight to preserve
their independence.**

ΔΕΙ ΑΕΙ ΠΡΑΤΤΕΙΝ ΤΙ ΜΕΙΖΟΝ ΤΩΝ ΥΠΑΡΧΟΝΤΩΝ

Always seek something better
than what you have.

ΚΡΕΙΤΤΟΝ ΕΥΗΘΗ ΔΟΚΕΙΝ Η ΠΟΝΗΡΟΝ ΕΙΝΑΙ

Better to be considered
stupid than base.

ΔΕΙ ΤΟΝ ΕΥ ΦΡΟΝΟΥΝΤΑ ΤΟΝ ΛΟΓΙΣΜΟΝ ΑΕΙ ΤΩΝ ΕΠΙΘΥΜΙΩΝ ΚΡΕΙΤΤΩ ΠΕΙΡΑΣΘΑΙ ΠΟΙΕΙΝ

A man with sound
judgement must always
impose reason over desire.

ΤΟ ΦΥΛΑΞΑΙ Τ'ΑΓΑΘΑ ΤΟΥ ΚΤΗΣΑΣΘΑΙ ΧΑΛΕΠΩΤΕΡΟΝ

It is more difficult to keep goods
than to acquire them.

ΟΥΔΕΙΣ ΑΥΤΟΣ ΑΥΤΟΥ ΚΑΤΗΓΟΡΗΣΕ ΠΩΠΟΤΕ

Nobody ever denounced himself.

His life

Demosthenes was born in Athens and died on the island of Calauria, now called Poros. His father, whose name was also Demosthenes, was the owner of two enterprises; in one of them he made swords and knives, and in the other upholstery. Demosthenes' father died when the orator was a child. His guardians abused their trust by squandering his father's fortune. Later he brought an unsuccessful court action against them to recover it, which at the same time gave him an opportunity to acquire considerable experience as an orator. The lack of appropriate guardianship contributed to the young Demosthenes' neglect of education. In addition to this misfortune, he suffered from some physical disabilities that did little to help him become a good orator: he had a speech impediment, and his breathing was so weak he could not recite an entire verse without taking a breath. In addition he was physically unattractive and sickly, which was why he did not engage in physical education, as did most young men in Athens then

But he overcame his physical defects and developed into a powerful orator.

Demosthenes appeared in the public life of Athens when the city had to confront the expansionist designs of Philip the Macedon; but the Athenians were listless and irresolute, because they were divided. Some believed that all Hellenes should join together under the sceptre of the Macedonian king, and others objected to this in the belief that this would be tantamount to Athens' subjugation to Philip

Demosthenes belonged to the latter group, and for this reason used his rhetorical power to lift the spirits of the Athenians and urged them to resist Philip and later his son Alexander.

For 15 years he fought against Philip. In his *Philippics* and *Olynthiacs* he tried to alert the Athenians to what he perceived as the threat of the Macedon.

His involvement in political quarrels and charges of impropriety against him obliged him to leave Athens. After being convicted and imprisoned, he escaped and sought refuge in the temple of Poseidon in Poros, where he committed suicide by taking poison rather than die by the sword.

His work

Some 61 speeches attributed to Demosthenes have been preserved, as well as 56 sketches of political speeches and six epistles. Some of these speeches are forensic and others political. We shall examine the content of the more important ones below.

The speech *To Leptines* was delivered in 355 BC by Demosthenes, who was advocate for two Athenians who had violated a law proposed by Leptines. In accordance with this law, no citizen should be untaxed. Demosthenes argued that the two men in question should continue to enjoy their tax-free status because they provided significant diplomatic services.

In the following year (354 BC) he wrote *Against Androtion,* a speech against Androtion, pupil of Isocrates. Androtion had proposed that a golden crown be awarded to the outgoing Boule of 500 as an honour, even though the Boule had not been able to build the previously determined number of new ships. His real purpose was to nudge out Androtion politically, as the latter had become unpopular because of his collection of taxes.

His speech *Against Timocrates* had a similar purpose. It was against a law that would help those who had embezzled money from the state, including Androtion, to avoid the penalties. A large part of *Against Timocrates* was taken, almost word for word, from his speech *Against Androtion,* which shows that the attack was in the same vein.

These three speeches were forensic in nature.

The first political speech by Demosthenes was *On the Navy Boards,* about increasing the taxation of the wealthy to re-equip the fleet. He spoke at the Assembly of the people and proposed that the number of citizens who should contribute be increased from 1200 to 2000. The speech was delivered in 354 and from that date on, Demosthenes dedicated almost all his energies to his political career.

Two political speeches followed, each of which concerned a critical problem of foreign policy. In *For the people of Megalopolis,* which was delivered at the end of 353, he advises the deme of the Athenians to help the Arcadians resist attacks by the Lacedaemonians, so as not to upset the balance of forces in the Peloponnese to the benefit of Lacedaemon (Sparta).

In his speech *For the Rhodians,* delivered in 352 BC, the orator recommends that the city assist the democrats on Rhodes who were being oppressed by the oligarchs, by supporting King Mausolus of Caria. This would have been quite difficult to achieve because these same democrats had been convinced by Mausolus to break away from the Athenian Confederacy, and were thus accomplices in the failure of the second naval alliance.

In this speech, Demosthenes formulated for the first time the principle to which he remained faithful throughout the rest of his life, i.e. that Athenians should become "common protectors of every city's freedom".

At the same time he pointed out that the enemy most to be feared by the Athenians was not the King of the Persians, but Philip the Macedon.

His speech *Against Aristocrates* was delivered in the courts by Euthycleas of Thrace in 352 BC. In it, Demosthenes reports on developments in Thrace; his goal was to prepare for resistance against Philip, who had begun to move toward the Hellespont with a view to obtaining control of the Straits. Culminating Demosthenes' anti-Macedonian stance were the three *Philippics.*

The *First Philippic* is an appeal for resistance. It is a cry of alarm in the hope of creating a national army prepared to intervene wherever necessary. A similar case is made in the *First Olynthiac,* to defend Olynthus, a large town in Chalcidice. Demosthenes showed that this was the pre-eminent opportunity. So he asked that help be sent to Olynthus, but also recommended reform of the *Theoric Fund,* making remarks about the financial policy of Eubulus, who as head of the Fund from 350 to 345 BC, had excerised control over Athenian finances and maintained a pacific attitude toward Philip.

With his *Second Philippic,* Demosthenes sought to maintain the spirit of distrust that prevailed against the king of Macedonia.

He said that Philip "while pleading peace, is in fact planning war against the Athenians, as can be seen from his collaboration with the Thebans and his effort to annex cities in the Peloponnese".

He uses similar arguments in all the *Philippics* and in the three *Olynthiacs*, all of which advised, recommended, warned, urged, and accused.

From the period of Dionysios of Halicarnassus (1st c. BC) on, Demosthenes was recognised as the foremost orator in ancient Greece. His contemporary Athenians acknowledged the services he offered the city by awarding him a golden crown and acquitting Ctesiphon at the trial held in 330 BC. At this trial, Demosthenes delivered his speech *On the Crown*, which is the vindication of his policy.

The essence of his political thought was respect for the law and the willingness of the people to assume their responsibilities.

ΤΟ ΓΑΡ ΕΥ ΠΡΑΤΤΕΙΝ ΠΑΡΑ ΤΗΝ ΑΞΙΑΝ ΑΦΟΡΜΗΝ
ΤΟΥ ΚΑΚΩΣ ΦΡΟΝΕΙΝ ΤΟΙΣ ΑΝΟΗΤΟΙΣ ΓΙΓΝΕΤΑΙ

Success without value is an occasion for silly people to think badly.

ΠΟΝΗΡΟΝ Ο ΣΥΚΟΦΑΝΤΗΣ ΑΕΙ

The sycophant is always malevolent.

ΕΠΕΙΔΑΝ ΑΠΑΝΤ' ΑΚΟΥΣΗΤΕ ΚΡΙΝΑΤΕ

Judge after hearing everything.

LYCURGUS

390-323 BC

**Athenian orator and politician.
As an orator, he wrote mainly forensic
speeches, particularly impeachments.
He was faithful to traditional Athenian principles,
which he supported zealously in his rhetorical practice as well.
He showed particular abilities as an economist
and as financial manager of Athens.**

ΠΑΝΤΩΝ ΕΣΤΙΝ ΔΥΣΧΕΡΕΣΤΑΤΟΝ ΤΟ ΠΟΛΛΟΙΣ ΑΡΕΣΚΕΙΝ

Pleasing the many is the most difficult task of all.

**An excerpt from the conclusion of his oration "Against Leocrates"
Leocrates conveys the rhetorical style of Lycurgus:**

"Thus I accuse Leocrates before you, who have the competence to punish him both
as judges and in the name of the gods ... Leocrates is guilty of all offences: treason,
because by abandoning the city, he left it a pawn to its enemies; abolition of the
democratic political system because he failed to endure the threat to freedom; impiety
because as much as he was able, he left the shrines and temples of the gods to be
destroyed; impiety to parents, because he allowed their monuments to be eliminated
and deprived them of the usual honours; desertion and insubordination because he failed
to present himself upon the call of the homeland and to report for service to the generals.
After all this, who would want to acquit him? Who is so good that he would
wish to save him, and leave his own salvation to the mood of those who are always ready
to abandon us. Who will agree, out of pity for him, to abandon his country to the mercy of
the enemy, who will not feel any compassion, and thus will destroy us?
And who will agree to expose himself to the vengeance of the gods
in order to show mercy to the betrayer of his country?"

**... But the Athenian judges acquitted Leocrates,
by the admittedly slender majority of one vote.**

His life

Athenian orator and politician, just a few years older than Demosthenes. Scion of an old Athenian family, he was a faithful follower of the principles characteristic of the old-time Athenians: devotion to religion and the gods of the city; austerity in private life, an unforgiving stance to anyone who betrayed the city or breached the established ethical and political rules. His faith in these principles was so strong that Lycurgus can be said to place his rhetoric at the service of his moral and political ideals. He was a pupil of Plato and Isocrates, and together with Demosthenes, headed the fight against the Macedonians. Although Lycurgus was active as an orator and politician, as pointed out earlier, he distinguished himself primarily in internal organisation and finance. He entered politics at an advanced age. We find him in 340 BC cooperating with Demosthenes in cleaning up the administration of Athens.

For twelve years, from 338 to 326 BC, he managed the finances of the city with great success and then beautified the city by repairing walls, building a stadium and a gymnasium, completing the arsenal, reconstructing the great theatre of Dionysus and fostering various works of art.

After the battle of Chaeronea, he supported the military preparation of the city and fought, together with Demosthenes and Hypereides, to organise the Athenians' defence against Philip II. At that time 650 talents were collected from optional contributions in order to arm the fleet and strengthen the public treasury.

His work

As an orator, Lycurgus does not appear to have been gifted with any particularly strong talent for rhetoric.

He wrote 15 speeches that were forensic in their entirety and, in particular, impeachments. In two of these he was defending himself in trials of accountability. Just one of his speeches has been preserved in its entirety, *Against Leocrates,* in which he accused the Athenian Leocrates of treason because after the battle of Chaeronea, Leocrates in a panic fled secretly for Rhodes, taking with him his money and his family. From there he went to Megara, where he remained for more than five years, and then returned to Athens, hoping that his case would have been forgotten. Lycurgus immediately filed charges against him, but Leocrates was acquitted.

The truth is that the charge against Leocrates was not based so much on specific laws relative to Leocrates' particular behaviour, as on Lycurgus' general view of the duties of the citizen, which he artfully linked with the glorious past of the city, quoting many extracts from the classical period. This speech is a veritable anthology.

ΟΥ ΠΟΙΗΣΟΜΑΙ ΠΕΡΙ ΠΛΕΙΟΝΟΣ ΤΟ ΖΗΝ ΤΗΣ ΕΛΕΥΘΕΡΙΑΣ

I would not choose life over liberty.

ISOCRATES

436 -338 BC

One of the greatest, best known
Athenian orators of the
4th century BC. He wrote forensic,
advisory and showpiece speeches.
In them he urged the Greeks to
make peace among themselves
and join together to fight
the barbarians; for this reason they
are regarded as exemplary expressions
of high sentiments, patriotism
and Hellenism.

Α ΠΟΙΕΙΝ ΑΙΣΧΡΟΝ
ΤΑΥΤΑ ΝΟΜΙΖΕ ΜΗΔΕ
ΛΕΓΕΙΝ ΕΙΝΑΙ ΚΑΛΟΝ

Whatever is shameful to do
should not even be uttered.

ΑΓΑΠΑ ΤΩΝ ΑΓΑΘΩΝ
ΜΗ ΤΗΝ
ΥΠΕΡΒΑΛΛΟΥΣΑΝ ΚΤΗΣΙΝ
ΑΛΛΑ ΤΗΝ ΜΕΤΡΙΑΝ
ΑΠΟΛΑΥΣΙΝ

Be not fond of acquiring goods,
and enjoy them in moderation.

ΒΡΑΔΕΩΣ ΜΕΝ ΦΙΛΟΣ
ΓΙΓΝΟΥ ΓΕΝΟΜΕΝΟΣ ΔΕ
ΠΕΙΡΩ ΔΙΑΜΕΝΕΙΝ

Be slow to make friends,
but having done so,
strive to remain a friend.

ΜΙΣΕΙ ΤΟΥΣ
ΚΟΛΑΚΕΥΟΝΤΑΣ ΩΣΠΕΡ
ΤΟΥΣ ΕΞΑΠΑΤΟΥΝΤΑΣ

Hate flatterers precisely
as you would hate crooks.

ΠΕΡΙ ΠΛΕΙΟΝΟΣ ΠΟΙΟΥ
ΔΟΞΑΝ ΚΑΛΗΝ Η
ΠΛΟΥΤΟΝ ΜΕΓΑ
ΤΟΙΣ ΠΑΙΣΙ ΚΑΤΑΛΙΠΕΙΝ

Better to leave
your children a good name
than great wealth.

His life and work

He was born in the town of Erchia, east of Athens, the son of Theodoros, a prosperous maker of flutes. His family's affluence made it possible for him to be educated by the most famous rhetoricians and Sophists of the age. He attended classes given by Socrates but without following his teachings systematically.

The mind of Isocrates must have impressed Socrates, because we can see in the epilogue to the Platonic dialogue *Phaedrus* that the great teacher prophesied a brilliant future for the young Isocrates, were he to take up rhetoric or philosophy. As Isocrates himself notes, his natural shyness and weak voice prevented him from becoming involved in public affairs or being active as a political orator.

Early in his career, he worked for eight years as a *logographos*, writing speeches for other people to give at court. But this work did not suit him and in 393 BC, he opened a school of rhetoric on Chios. Three years later, he established a school of rhetoric or, as he himself used to call it, a school of philosophy, in Athens. But Isocrates did not use the word philosophy in the sense of engagement with metaphysical problems, but rather in the sense of cultivating the mind as a whole, strengthening the character, shaping sound judgement and developing the greatest of human features, the language.

Isocrates' school became a university. Pupils came from all towns to study there, including many important men, politicians, historians and orators. Isocrates had the ability to see political affairs in Greece objectively. In his speeches he advised the Greeks to join together against the enemy. The battle of Chaeronea in 338 was a heavy blow for old Isocrates, who was then 98 years old. Five days after the battle, he died of sorrow. He was buried at public expense, and a Siren was placed on his grave, as a symbol of the attractive grace of his face and personality.

Of all of Isocrates' speeches, six forensic speeches have come down to us, eight letters and 14 showpiece and advisory speeches.

His forensic speeches were entitled *Before the Aeginetan Court, On Banking, About the Chariot, To Callimachus, Against Lochetus,* and *To those Responsible.*

His advisory and showpiece speeches bore the titles: *Encomium of Helen, Busiris, To Plataea, Archidamus, On the Areopagus, On the Exchange, To Philip, Panathenaic, Panegyric, Against the Sophists, On Peace, To Nicocles,* and *Evagoras.*

ΠΕΝΙΑ ΤΕΧΝΑΣ ΑΠΕΡΓΑΖΕΤΑΙ

Poverty finds many means of survival.

ISOCRATES' WORKS

A. FORENSIC SPEECHES

Before the Aeginetan Court: Speech before the courts of Aegina about an inheritance case. This is the speech that was most admired by all and the only forensic oration written for courts outside Athens to have been preserved from the classical period.

On Banking: Speech about a metic (resident alien) who found himself in need and asked the banker Pasionas to give him collateral.

On the Chariot: Written for Alcibiades, whose father's name was also Alcibiades. The speech contained a eulogy for the father Alcibiades, a brilliant encomium full of affectation and exaggeration. Someone had accused the father of having borrowed a chariot to take part in chariot races, and of failing to return it after the victory. The trial was postponed many times, the father Alcibiades died and, when his son came of age, he had to give an account on his father's behalf against the charges that had been levelled against him.

To Callimachus: This speech refers to a case of political limitation, the main part of which is praise for the amnesty of 403 BC, which gives his speech political significance. Throughout his life, Isocrates was an ardent champion of national unity, and saw the exemplary reconciliation of 403 as one of Athens's greatest moments

Against Lochetus: He accuses a wealthy young man of having mistreated a poor citizen. It is a strong homily against violence, which emphasises that force must be suppressed.

To Those Responsible: Speech delivered at a trial in which a citizen demanded the return of money paid. The speech is called "unwitnessed" because neither of the two adversaries presented witnesses. It has been preserved only in note form.

B. SHOWPIECE – ADVISORY SPEECHES

Encomium to Helen: Written as a showpiece to be used at his school, it shows that Isocrates believes themes of this kind should be developed. Using rhetorical exaggeration, a good many absurdities and sophistries, he attempts to defend the morality of Helen of Troy, arguing that she behaved as she should have done and deserves only commendation. What justified Helen was her beauty -about which Isocrates had such high praise that it became famous- a divine gift that surpassed all others and was higher than the other powers of her soul.

Busiris: Busiris was a mythic king or tyrant in Egypt. As in the case of Helen, Isocrates defends the accused by speaking of the noble and lofty themes that can be associated with his person, avoiding any mention of his crimes. It is said that the Egyptian tyrant would every year sacrifice the life of a guest foreigner to appease the gods. Isocrates deplores the "blasphemy of the poets" who attribute many scandals to gods and heroes.

To Plataea: A strongly worded advisory speech. It is assumed to have been delivered by an inhabitant of Plataea to the Athenian Ecclesia (Assembly) of the Deme in 373 BC, after his homeland was destroyed by the Thebans. It describes the atrocities of the Thebans and advises the Athenians to help the unfortunate Plataeans return to their homeland.

Archidamus: Quite similar to the Plataea speech. During a meeting held in Sparta, the heir to the throne Archidamus talks about the peace terms offered by Thebes in 366 BC. The speech expresses the feelings appropriate to the Spartans and the stance adopted by Sparta was, in fact, that argued by Archidamus.

On the Areopagus: Concerns the internal situation in Athens, and contains a proposal to cure the sufferings caused by the so-called Social War. A return to moderate oligarchy and aristocratic institutions would give Athens back its old prestige, according to Isocrates.

On the Exchange: This is the longest of Isocrates's speeches, which he wrote at the age of 82. It was the defence in an imaginary trial. It is hypothesised that Lysimachus, who regarded Isocrates as wealthier than himself because he made a great deal of money from teaching rhetoric, proposed that Isocrates undertake to outfit a trireme or to exchange their properties, as stipulated by Attic law. This was the "exchange" in question.

To Philip: This is more of an epistle than an oration. When Isocrates realised that Athens and Sparta were unable to rally the Greeks together in a joint campaign against the Persians, he turned his attention to addressing individual persons such as Dionysius of Syracuse, Archidamus of Sparta, and Philip of Macedonia and invited them to become champions of the national idea.

Panathenaic: One of the longest and perhaps best speeches by Isocrates written just three years before the wise teacher of rhetoric would have reached his 100th birthday. In it, with justified self-satisfaction, he boasts that he still feels the intellectual concerns of his youth. Panathenaic is something like Isocrates' political will and testament.

Panegyric: In this, his first and most significant work, Isocrates urged the Greeks to unite politically in a joint military campaign in the East. Isocrates believed that with a panhellenic war against the Persians, the political fragmentation of Greece could be overcome and a solution found to social problems such as poverty. From one viewpoint, which has many supporters, the Panegyric contains two speeches simultaneously, one showpiece and one advisory. The showpiece part describes Athens with its great accomplishments, and in the advisory part it proposes the unification of the Greeks against the barbarians under the leadership of Athens and Sparta.

Against the Sophists: Isocrates published this speech in 393 BC, when he founded his school; thus it was at the same time a manifesto and a libel. It was a manifesto of the educational programme of his school and a libel against his two special enemies: sowers of discord and Sophists.

On Peace: He tries to convince the Athenians that they should abandon the dreams of Athens' naval supremacy and treat other Greeks as equals and not as subjects.

To Nicocles: Addressed to the young Cypriot leader Nicocles who had just succeeded to the throne of his deceased father; it explains the duties of the king and how the kingdom should be run. It is an admonitory speech in essence, that analyses the meaning of the monarchy. In it, the monarch himself is supposed to be talking to Nicocles, and reminding his subjects of their duties as well.

Evagoras: This is an encomium to a dead king and, at the same time, a description of the ideal leader, of whom Evagoras was the most perfect embodiment. In Isocrates' view, the intellectually and morally integrated leader is a beneficent force in the city, always giving a good example and educating the citizens.

Aesop, top of a plate.
Lateran Museum, Rome.

AESOP

6th century BC

He was the inventor of fables, in which adults and children alike could learn through the use of clever allegories. The fables were not written, but recited. Aesop's fables, which are well known to this day, were revised in the 14th century by the Greek monk Maximus Planudes.

ΟΜΟΝΟΙΑΝ ΧΡΩΜΕΝΟΙΣ ΣΩΤΗΡΙΟΝ

Concord is a salutary thing
for those who use it.

ΤΟΥΣ ΦΡΟΝΙΜΟΥΣ ΔΕΙ
ΠΡΟΤΕΡΟΝ ΣΚΟΠΕΙΝ ΤΑ
ΤΕΛΗ ΤΩΝ ΠΡΑΓΜΑΤΩΝ ΕΙΘ´
ΟΥΤΩΣ ΑΥΤΟΙΣ ΕΠΙΧΕΙΡΕΙΝ

Sensible people must first consider
the result of their action
and only then carry it out.

ΜΗ ΜΕΜΦΟΥ ΠΛΗΝ
ΕΛΕΗΣΟΝ

Do not criticise but assist.

Ο ΤΗΣ ΦΙΛΟΔΟΞΙΑΣ ΕΡΩΣ
ΤΩΝ ΑΝΘΡΩΠΩΝ ΝΟΥΝ
ΕΠΙΘΟΛΟΙ

Ambition muddies the mind of man.

ΤΟΥ ΣΩΜΑΤΙΚΟΥ ΚΑΛΛΟΥΣ
ΑΜΕΙΝΩΝ ΕΣΤΙ Ο ΤΗΣ
ΔΙΑΝΟΙΑΣ ΚΟΣΜΟΣ

Beauty of the mind is superior
to that of the body.

ΣΥΝ ΑΘΗΝΑ ΚΑΙ ΧΕΙΡΑ ΚΙΝΕΙ

The gods help those who help themselves.

His life and work

Aesop lived in the 6th century BC; he came from Asia Minor, and his life is full of legend. It is said that he was a slave from Phrygia who lived during the era of the Seven Wise Men, whom he knew personally. His biography is embellished with many anecdotes and legends. The book entitled *The Life of Aesop* contains information that is clearly fictitious and implausible, casting doubt as to his very existence and causing some people to deny it altogether.

Nevertheless Aesop existed. He was initially a slave purchased by the Samian philosopher Xanthus, who then sold him to another Samian sage named Iadmon. Iadmon appreciated Aesop's mental gifts, his wisdom and intelligence, and gave him his freedom. As a free man, Aesop lived in Samos where he was held in high esteem. Later he went to Sardis to the court of King Croesus. He also travelled to Egypt. He is reported to have been ugly, hunchbacked and a mute. It is also reported that Xanthus's wife was frightened when she saw the new slave her husband had brought home.

Some 359 fables have been preserved under Aesop's name, most of which are ingenuous and charming.In them, animals usually speak and act as though they were human; on occasion, the heroes are humans and gods, and in a few they are even plants. All the fables are delightful to read for their originality and fresh charm. The edifying is intermixed with the enjoyable and they all end with some moral lesson, easy to understand and applicable to adults and children alike. The fables were appropriate for every occasion and for this reason were widely known. They added spice to discussions and writings. Such fables can be found in Archilochus, Hesiod, and Theognis. Aesop did not write his fables.

Together with the old fables that he had stored in his memory, he would compose new ones in his mind and at the right moment would narrate them, sometimes at gatherings of ordinary people and sometimes in the mansions of the wealthy. He had a great talent in devising and narrating fables, which was why his fame spread so far. Fabulists such as the Romans Babrius, Phaedrus and Avianos wrote poetic adaptations of Aesop's fables, and we encounter imitations of them in antiquity in the works of orators and philosophers.

It appears that Aesop met his death in a violent episode in Delphi. According to versions of the story found in various authors, he was killed by the inhabitants of Delphi by being pushed off a high rock, either because he made fun of them for not working the land – which was barren – but expecting to live from the offerings of strangers to the sanctuary of Apollo, or because he refused to give them a considerable sum of money which Croesus, king of Lydia, had sent with Aesop as an offering to the god. Aesop did not hand the money over because, it is said, he regarded them as unworthy of gifts.

ARCHIMEDES

287-212 BC

**The first inventor of antiquity.
He was also an important mathematician,
engineer and astronomer.
His writings include significant
works of mathematics.**

ΔΩΣ ΜΟΙ ΠΑ ΣΤΩ ΚΑΙ ΤΑΝ ΓΑΝ ΚΙΝΑΣΩ

Give me a firm spot on which to stand and I will move the earth.

His life

Archimedes was a multi-faceted personality: mathematician, inventor, engineer and astronomer. He was also one of the most distinguished wise men of antiquity, founder of theoretical mechanics and the greatest inventor of his age.

He was born in Syracuse and died when the Roman army under General Marcellus captured Syracuse and slaughtered its inhabitants. Tradition says that Archimedes was killed while absorbed in trying to find the solution to a problem. The same tradition reports that he confronted the Roman soldier with the famous phrase "Don't disturb the circles".

He is believed to have been the son of the astronomer Pheidias. Allhough he was one of the greatest minds in antiquity, we know very little about him He was reported to have been a pupil of Euclid, to have travelled in Egypt and studied in Alexandria. Eventually, he returned to Syracuse where he wrote most of his works.

His work

The works of Archimedes prove that he had an extremely good background in the mathematics and astronomy of his age. On some issues he is regarded as a precursor not only of Newton and Leibnitz, but also of Riemann. This is why it has been said that anyone who understands Archimedes is less impressed with the inventions and achievements of modern wise men.

His fame is due both to his accomplishments in mechanics and to his writing of mathematical works

To the first category belong devices such as the Archimedes screw for raising water, a machine for transferring large loads, and the war machines that he devised to reinforce the defence of his city against Marcellus

He wrote mathematical works of major significanco, a good many of which are extant. From the titles of his works alone, the reader will grasp the breadth of Archimedes' experiments and thinking in the field of mathematics, astronomy, mechanics, etc.

Archimedes exhibited originality of thought in his mathematical proofs and presentations, as well as rigour of the highest modern standards. Particularly with respect to mathematics, Archimedes was the pioneer of the modern age. Every four years, mathematicians from all over the world gather together at the World Conference of the International Mathematical Association to pay homage to the most outstanding works of young scientists. The figure of Archimedes is depicted on the medal awarded on this occasion (the equivalent of the Nobel Prize for mathematics).

The following are Archimedes's extant treatises, with a brief description of each one.

«The death of Archimedes». Copy of 3rd cent. BC
Roman mosaic (Frankfurt, Municipal Institute of Art).

ARCHIMEDES' WORKS

On the Sphere and Cylinder (in two books):
The object of the study is the sphere, the cone, and the cylinder. The work contains 44 theorems in the first book and nine problems in the second.

Measurement of the Circle:
Includes theorems related to the geometric dimensions of the circle. The most important is the one in which the ratio of the circumference to the diameter of a circle is shown to lie between 3 1/7and 3 10/71, the famous Π = 3.14.

On Conoids and Spheroids:
This book consists of a total of 32 theorems dealing with the segments of solids formed by the revolution of a conic section about its axis. One of the most important results is the discovery of the formula for calculating the area of an ellipse.

On Spirals:
The systematic study of the geometric properties of tangents to the spiral of Archimedes, from the point of view of analytic geometry and of differential and integral calculus.

On the Equilibrium of Planes or the Centres of Gravity of Planes:
Treatise referring to the centres of gravity of various rectilinear planes and their definition. This is the first systematic foundation for theoretical mechanics.

Quadrature of the Parabola:
It is proved, using first mechanical and then geometric methods, that the area of any segment of a parabola is equal to 3/4 of the area of any inscribed triangle with the same base and height.

On Floating Bodies:
This treatise was written in two books. The first establishes what has become known as the Archimedes principle of hydrostatics. In the second he determines the various positions of stability assumed by a right paraboloid of revolution when floating in a fluid of greater specific gravity.

The Sand-Reckoner:
A place-value system of notation to express very large numbers. Archimedes used this as a basis on which to calculate the number of grains of sand required to fill the whole universe. He found it to be about 10^{63}.

Method Concerning Mechanical Theorem:
This book is of great interest because in it Archimedes explains how he arrived at many of his discoveries in mathematics by using a "mechanical" method.

Cattle Problem:
A text in the Ionian dialect consisting of 44 verses. It is about calculating the number of cattle belonging to the god Helios that grazed on the island of Thrinacia, according to Homer. It poses a problem in indeterminate analysis with eight unknowns, and has not been solved.

In Arabic translation:
The following works have been ascribed to Archimedes: Inscribing a regular heptagon in a circle, On touching circles, Principles of Geometry and On hydraulic clocks. In addition to these, subsequent authors report other books which have not come down to us, such as On triangles, On rectangles, On the 13 semicanonical polyhedra, Arithmetic, On catoptrics, the Stomachion, and others. Archimedes' authorship of these works has been disputed.

HERODOTUS
484 -410 BC

Called "the father of history",
Herodotus was the first to transform
history into knowledge as he separated
the information he collected in order
to be sure it was used in the best,
most objective possible way
in the recording of history.

ΚΑΔΜΕΙΑ ΝΙΚΗ

Pyrrhic victory.

ΠΡΙΝ ΑΝ ΤΕΛΕΥΤΗΣΗ
ΕΠΙΣΧΕΙΝ ΜΗΔΕ
ΚΑΛΕΕΙΝ ΚΩ ΟΛΒΙΟΝ

No man can be called happy
until he dies.

ΩΤΑ ΓΑΡ ΤΥΓΧΑΝΕΙ
ΑΝΘΡΩΠΟΙΣΟΙ
ΕΟΝΤΑ ΑΠΙΣΤΟΤΕΡΑ
ΟΦΘΑΛΜΩΝ

The ears are less reliable
witnesses than the eyes.

ΩΣ ΚΥΚΛΟΣ ΤΩΝ
ΑΝΘΡΩΠΗΤΩΝ ΕΣΤΙ
ΠΡΗΓΜΑΤΩΝ

The affairs of man are
cyclical by nature.

Η ΙΣΗΓΟΡΙΗ ΩΣ ΕΣΤΙ
ΧΡΗΜΑ ΣΠΟΥΔΑΙΟΝ

Freedom of speech is an important thing.

His life

Herodotus was born in Halicarnassus in Asia Minor, lived on Samos, returned to Halicarnassus, went to Athens and ended up in the Athenian colony of Thurii in southern Italy near the devastated town of Sybaris. He was among the most travelled of all previous writers, and these traces left their effect on his multi-faceted work. The incentive for his travels was his desire to see new places and people.

Among the people he met and kept company with in Athens were Pericles, Protagoras and Sophocles; with the latter he had a close friendship.

His work

Herodotus classified the information contained in his work into three categories:

a) what he himself saw,

b) what he was told by eyewitnesses, and

c) what he learned from hearsay alone. His systematic classification of information is what has made him recognised as a serious historian.

His *History* of the Persian Wars is divided into nine books, each of which bears the name of one of the nine Muses. This division appears to have been made by an Alexandrine scholar rather than by Herodotus himself, but it is considered successful. The length of the books is not uniform because the obvious criterion was the internal conceptual units of the work and the weight that the author attaches to each of the historical events he sets out.

Herodotus' history is a work of inestimable value. Most of what we know about the ancient world up to the Persian wars, but after them as well, we owe to this work. It is a reliable source and the only continuous and complete work extant about an important era in history. He was truly «the father of history», as Cicero called him.

In his *History*, Herodotus not only describes the strange things he saw and learned, he also passes on historical material about the political, military and cultural history of ancient peoples. This was his goal, even though he arrives at it indirectly and by means of digressions.

Herodotus is regarded as having been unjustly treated by history, because he is always compared with Thucydides, who justifiably takes first place. But Herodotus has always been read, and has always had admirers and imitators.

The fact that his history, an extensive and difficult text owing to the language he uses, has been preserved in its entirety -whereas so many others have been lost- is sufficient proof of the fact that he was esteemed by both his contemporaries and by subsequent scholars alike.

In fact, since his work is the first historical text in Europe with breadth in the content and with broad enough boundaries in terms of both place and time to give us a panoramic view of the history and culture of the known world at that time, it is placed at the beginning of European history and thus he is regarded as the first European historian.

HERODOTUS' WORK

Book I Clio:
Describes the reasons for the conflict between the Hellenes and the barbarians, the story of the creation of the Persian state of Croesus, Cyrus and the conquests of the Persians.

Book II Euterpe:
Includes the kingdom of Cambysis, the campaign against Egypt and facts about the Egyptians.

Book III Thalia:
Supplements the information about the kingdom of Cambysis and refers to the conquest of Egypt, Cyrene, and Libya, the expedition against the Ethiops and that of the Corinthians and Spartans against Polycrates, tyrant of Samos.

Book IV Melpomene:
Describes Darius' unfortunate campaign to Scythia, the capture of Thrace by the Persians and the campaign to Libya.

Book V Terpsichore:
Includes the subjugation of Thrace, Byzantium, Carthage, Imbros, etc. by the Persians, and the Ionian uprising that had such serious repercussions. In this book there are many digressions about the history of neighbouring peoples so that the book consists of many small chapters about Phrygia, Caria, the Hellespont and Cyprus.

Book VI Erato:
Speaks of the crushing of the Ionian uprising, the fall and destruction of Miletus, the first unsuccessful campaign by Mardonius against Greece, the battle of Marathon and the defeat of the Persians

Book VII Polymnia:
Refers to the death of Darius, the rise of Xerxes to the throne, his campaign against Greece, the organisation of the Greek resistance and the battle of Thermopylae.

Book VIII Urania:
Narrates the naval battle at Artemision, the descent of the Persians, the naval battle of Salamis, the defeat of the Persians on land and at sea, and Xerxes' flight.

Book IX Calliope:
Speaks of Maradonius's invasion of Attica, the battle of Plataea, the battle of Mycale and the capture of Sestos on the Hellespont in 478 BC by the Athenians. In the last chapter of Book IX, Herodotus tells a story by way of an epilogue: A discussion was taking place between Cyrus and Artembaris, a Persian noble, who advised Cyrus to abandon Persia for a new homeland, fertile and wealthy. Cyrus pretends to agree, but advises all of those who shared the opinion of Artembaris:"Be prepared not to rule but to be ruled by others, because in wealthy countries men become soft".
"The same country will never be able to produce splendid fruit and brave warriors".

PAUSANIAS

2nd century AD

His life and work

This Greek traveller was born in Magnesia in Asia Minor, south of Troy, and appears to have been well off, was very fond of travelling and anxious to learn. This is why he travelled widely in Asia Minor, Syria, Egypt, Greece, Italy, Palestine and Arabia, as well as the Western Mediterranean. He gathered his impressions from all his voyages in a work divided into 10 books under the general title *Description of Greece*, which has been preserved in its entirety. The 10 books are: *Attica, Corinth, Laconia, Messenia, Elis* (2 books), *Achaea, Arcadia, Boeotia* and *Phocis*. Each of these books is devoted to one of the most important regions of mainland Greece and, according to chronological evidence, must have been written between 160 and 180 AD.

The writer's intention was to describe the venerable monuments of Hellenic antiquity, the sights worth seeing in Greece, and the characteristics of life in Hellas. Pausanias lists all the sights he encounters, such as statues, paintings, tombs, and sanctuaries. He records traditions, anecdotes, and the myths that are linked with them, frequently indulges in lengthy historical digressions, and notes the towns, rivers and streets he encounters.

He talks about strange customs and superstitions or sometimes about the landscape and the natural products of the places he describes. He goes into particular detail in his description of the monuments of Athens, Olympia and Delphi.

The majority of what Pausanias narrates is based on personal experiences and on-the-spot evidence provided by his local informants, priests and others. His information is reliable and in a good many cases has been confirmed by the findings of archaeological excavations.

Pausanias's Description of Greece is an extremely valuable source of topographical information about ancient Hellas, about the history of ancient Greek art and knowledge of antiquity more generally. It is a unique source for archaeological, mythological, historical, geographical and folkloric information.

According to anthropologist and classical scholar J.G. Frazer, had it not been for Pausanias, "the ruins of Greece would for the most part be a labyrinth without a clue, a riddle without an answer".

THUCYDIDES

460-395 BC

Thucydides was the greatest
historian of antiquity, owing to
the unique work he left for us:
the History of the Peloponnesian War.
In this work, Thucydides portrayed
all the repercussions of this devastating
war that paralysed the most important
cities of Hellenic antiquity, Athens
and Sparta, as well as the smaller ones
involved on both sides.

ΠΕΡΥΚΑΣΙΝ ΑΠΑΝΤΕΣ
ΚΑΙ ΙΔΙΑ ΚΑΙ ΔΗΜΟΣΙΑ
ΑΜΑΡΤΑΝΕΙΝ ΚΑΙ ΟΥΚ
ΕΣΕΙ ΝΟΜΟΣ ΟΣΤΙΣ
ΑΠΕΙΡΞΕΙ ΤΟΥΤΟΥ

All men by nature tend toward
wrong-doing in both private and
public life, and there is no law
that can prevent this.

ΤΟ ΚΑΛΩΣ ΑΡΧΕΙΝ
ΤΑΥΤΟ ΕΣΤΙ ΟΣ Δ᾽
ΑΝ ΤΗΝ ΠΑΤΡΙΔΑ
ΩΦΕΛΗΣΗ ΩΣ ΠΛΕΙΣΤΑ
Η ΕΚΩΝ ΕΙΝΑΙ ΜΗΔΕΝ
ΒΛΑΨΗ

The duty of the good leader
is to do as much good
as possible for his country,
or at least not to harm it willingly.

ΟΥ ΓΑΡ ΠΑΣΧΟΝΤΕΣ
ΕΥ ΑΛΛΑ ΔΡΩΝΤΕΣ
ΚΤΩΜΕΘΑ ΤΟΥΣ
ΦΙΛΟΥΣ

We acquire friends
by doing good, not
by having good done to us.

ΤΟ ΕΥΔΑΙΜΟΝ ΤΟ ΕΛΕΥΘΕΡΟΝ,
ΤΟ Δ᾽ΕΛΕΥΘΕΡΟΝ ΕΥΨΥΧΟΝ ΕΣΤΙ

The foundation of happiness is freedom;
that of freedom is courage.

His life

We have very little information about the life of Thucydides. He was born in Alimous, today called Alimos, one of the demes of Athens. His father's name was Olorus and his mother's Hegesipyle. On his father's side, Thucydides was somehow related to Miltiades. He was one of the few to have caught the plague in 430-429 and to have recovered. His wife was from Thrace and he himself inherited gold mines in the region of the Stry-mon, which were the source of his financial well-being and independence. Thus he was able to attend classes given by the Sophists and then to devote himself to lengthy historical research and to the writing of his work. Among his teachers were the philoso-pher Anaxagoras, the Sophists Gorgias and Prodicus, and the orator Antiphon.

The period during which Thucydides came of age was characterised by an asto-nishing intellectual ferment and a vibrant cultural climate. A corresponding maturity is reflected in his work, in which he appears to seek the truth in everything, be it tradition or an event of his own time, coolly and without condescension. Of the incidents in his life, the most important was his election to the post of strategos (general) in 424 BC. Entrusted with command of the fleet in the Thrace region opposite Thasos, he failed to prevent the Spartan general Brasidas from capturing Amphipolis. This mistake caused him to be recalled, accused of treason and sentenced to exile or self-exile, where he remained for 20 years. He returned to Athens after the war, in 404 BC.

Most of his exile he spent in Thrace where his goldmines were. But he also visited pla-ces in which important military operations had taken place in the Peloponnese and Sicily, and certainly Syracuse. As an exile, he was permitted to come into contact with the Spartans and their allies and to learn their views about various matters related to the war. He spent the last years of his life on his land in Thrace, where he continued to write. But his work was cut short by his sudden death under uncertain conditions.

His work

The only work we have by Thucydides is the *History of the Peloponnesian War*, the war in which, between 431 and 404 BC, two large Hellenic cities Athens and Sparta fought and mobilised almost all other Greek towns on one or the other side. This history contains events from the beginning of the war (431) up to 411. The events in the war after 411 are described by Xenophon in his *Hellenica*. It should be pointed out that, although it appears that the Peloponnesian war lasted for 27 years, one should, to be accurate, sub-tract the period of almost seven years that elapsed after the peace of Nicias in 421 BC. Seeing the total events of the war and its description as a "twenty-seven year war" was the view of Thucydides as a historian not as a chronicler. He believed that all the events of these 27 years should be included. Thucydides did not divide his work into books, nor did he even give it a title. Ancient grammarians divided it into eight books and gave it the title *Thucydides' History*.

Thucydides was the first historian who applied serious scientific methodology to the gathering of material and the interpretation of historical events. He believed that the historian's first duty was to verify the truth. He levels stern criticism at the historians who preceded him, without actually mentioning any names, for what he regarded as inaccuracies that demonstrated their superficiality. This was why he relied on the method of on-the-spot and direct knowledge of events or why he cross checked information about events in which he himself did not participate. At other times he turned to the sources, extracting information from a city's archives, from official records, resolutions, treaties, pacts, etc. and always evaluating them with rationalist criteria. He preclude any supernatural intervention in the evolution of historical conditions and rejects any moralising in setting out historic events. Whatever happens, the constant is man and his nature, which seeks power and personal gain. Thucydides is one of the most outstanding minds of all ages, and one of the greatest writers of antiquity. His influence on those who came after him was very great. Polybius always referred to him. Salustius had him as a role model. Nobody ever disputed his credibility and reliability.

THE WORK OF THUCYDIDES

Book i: The history of Hellas prior to the Peloponnesian war is related, together with Thucydides' thoughts on it, the methodological assessments and investigation of the immediate causes of the war with a review of the primary principles and evolution of the Athenian hegemony.

Book ii: The military events are described that took place between 431 and 421, when the peace of Nicias was concluded. It is worth noting that this book contains Pericles' funeral oration for those fallen in the first year of the war, the moving description of the terrible plague that struck a great blow against Athens, Pericles' speech to the Athenians in which he tries to persuade the people to accept his defence tactic, and the death of Pericles.

Book iii: Divided mainly between the episodes of Plataea and Mytilene; Plataea was a loyal city, which was to suffer a tragic fate. Mytilene was a city in revolt, and obliged Athens to consider the problem of whether or not to punish it.
Regarding Plataea, after a three-year siege, the city was obliged to surrender to the Spartans and after a «trial», 200 of its citizens were put to death, the women were sold into slavery and the city was destroyed.

Book iv: Thucydides describes the incident at Pylos, the successes of the Athenians at Sphacteria and Cythera and the victory of the Boeotians at Delios. In Sicily however, things went badly for the Athenians.

Book v: The death of Brasidas and Cleon at Amphipolis. The rest of Book v describes the events between the peace of Nicias (421) and the campaign in Sicily (415).

Books vi and vii: Describes the Athenians' great expedition to Sicily, up to the disaster of the summer of 413 BC.

Book viii: Thucydides continues to narrate events in Hellas and Asia Minor up to 411 BC, the end of the 21st summer of the war. He assesses the effects of the disaster in Sicily, speaks about the political change of 411, i.e. the government of the Four Hundred, and about its fall.

XENOPHON

426-355 BC

Ancient historian, philosopher
and general, he was famed for
his realistic approach to events
and the simplicity of his writing.
In particular, the Romans admired
his practical mind, while his clarity
of discourse made him one of the most
widely read of the classical writers.

ΟΜΟΝΟΙΑ ΜΕΓΙΣΤΟΝ
ΑΓΑΘΟΝ ΔΟΚΕΙ ΤΑΙΣ
ΠΟΛΕΣΙΝ ΕΙΝΑΙ

Concord is the greatest good
that can be given to cities.

ΟΥΚ ΕΣΤΙΝ ΕΥΡΕΙΝ
ΒΙΟΝ ΑΛΥΠΟΝ
ΕΝ ΟΥΔΕΝΙ

No life passes without sorrow.

ΟΥ ΓΑΡ ΕΣΤΙ
ΔΙΔΑΣΚΑΛΟΣ ΟΥΔΕΙΣ
ΚΡΕΙΤΤΩΝ ΑΝΑΓΚΗΣ

Necessity is the best teacher.

ΟΙ ΓΑΡ ΠΟΝΟΙ ΟΨΟΝ
ΤΟΙΣ ΑΓΑΘΟΙΣ

Labour is
the spice of wealth.

Η ΜΕΝ ΤΟΥ ΣΩΜΑΤΟΣ ΙΣΧΥΣ ΓΗΡΑΣΚΕΙ,
Η ΔΕ ΤΗΣ ΨΥΧΗΣ ΡΩΜΗ
ΑΓΗΡΑΣΤΟΣ ΕΣΤΙΝ

Physical strength grows old. Mental power, however, is ageless.

His life

Xenophon was born of well-to-do parents, and therefore able to engage in hunting and horseback-riding all his life. At the age of 18, he met Socrates and became an admirer of his. This admiration lasted his entire life.

In 401 BC, his friend Proxenus from Boeotia, who had gone to Sardis to take part in Cyrus's expedition against his brother Artaxerxes, invited Xenophon along to meet Cyrus the younger, satrap of Frygia. The campaign, in which Greek mercenaries took part, was a failure. Cyrus was killed. The commanders of the Greek mercenary force were also murdered and Xenophon was elected *strategos* (general), together with five others. In 400 BC, he succeeded, after overcoming many obstacles and hazards, in leading 10,000 Greek mercenaries from the depths of Asia to Trebizond and then to Byzantium. The book is called *Anabasis Kyrou* or *The Expedition of Cyrus*.

Xenophon sympathised with the Spartan political system. In 396 BC, when Agesilaus, king of Sparta, became commander of the expedition to liberate the Hellenic cities in Asia Minor from the Persian yoke, Xenophon once again took part. He likewise followed Agesilaus and his campaign in Boeotia in 384 BC and fought against the Thebans in the battle of Coronea. Athenians accused Xenophon of siding with the Spartans, sentenced him to exile and confiscated his property. Then he took refuge in Sparta where the Spartans offered him a large property near Olympia so that he could live off his income. He lived there for 20 years. Later the Elians took the property and obliged Xenophon to flee to Corinth where he died.

Meanwhile, his good relations were restored with the Athenians, who revoked the decree of his exile.

His work

Xenophon wrote works with a wide variety of content. They fall into three groups:

1. **Moral and political:** Which are the works in which he defends his teacher Socrates, i.e. *Apologia*, *Memorabilia* and *Symposium*, the works in which he sets out his personal opinions such as *Cyropaedia* or *The Constitution of Sparta, Ways and Means, Oeconomicus and Hieron*.
2. **Technical:** Which are *On Horsemanship, Cavalry Officer* and *On Hunting*.
3. **Historical:** Such as *the Anabasis, Hellenica* and *Agesilaus*.

The *Socratic* works of Xenophon are a collection of memories from the time he spent with the wise teacher and were inspired by his profound and life-long respect for Socrates. His purpose was to contribute to honouring the memory of Socrates by describing what he himself remembered or heard from others.

Cyropaedia is the work which, more than any other, reflects his personal views. The dominant idea in this work is that the art of ruling is an important and very difficult one and that a good leader or governor is he who has the ability to convince those being ruled to do whatever he asks of them. In Xenophon's opinion, Cyrus the Great (590-529 BC) was such a leader and his personal superiority must be attributed to his higher education. Thus the title *Cyropaedia* can be explained precisely by the importance that Xenophon attaches to early training.

The *Constitution of Sparta* is a treatise in praise of the Spartan political system..

In the short treatise *Ways and Means*, Xenophon recommends various measures to the Athenians to increase the city's revenues. This is a short work, but extremely interesting in investigating financial relations in ancient Athens.

Oeconomicus is perhaps the best of all Xenophon's works. It was the product of his experience as a landowner. In it he argues that there is a science of estate management that is based on agriculture.

Hieron is a dialogue between Hieron, tyrant of Syracuse, and the poet Simonides of Kea. In this work, which is the opposite of Agesilaus, the adverse aspects of one-man rule, or tyranny, are described.

Of his technical works, *On horsemanship* is addressed to a private horseman and offers practical advice about the purchase and training of horses, the equipping of the riders, etc.

In *Cavalry Officer*, useful technical instructions are provided to the commander of the cavalry, in order to improve the Athenian cavalry, while *On Hunting* praises and justifies hunting as training for war and contains much technical information and practical advice for training dogs.

Of his historic works, finally, the *Anabasis* is an actual diary of the march of the ten thousand, written with power and art. In it the writer quotes a great deal of geographic, topographic, ethnographic and other information about the history of those places and the topography of that period, i.e. about 401 BC.

Hellenica is divided, as is the *Anabasis*, into seven books, which constitute Xenophon's main historical work. It is a continuation of Thucydides' history and narrates events from 411 to 362 BC.

Agesilaus is among Xenophon's shorter works and is more in praise of King Agesilaus than an objectively written biography. He extols Agesilaus for his respect for the gods, his loyalty to friends, his simple way of life, his bravery in battle, his obedience to state power and the laws, his patriotism and good manners to his inferiors. In this work, Xenophon clearly shows his sympathy for oligarchic Sparta.

PLUTARCH

46-125 AD

Plutarch was a great historian, but not
in the strict sense of the word, as in his work
he proves to be an equally great encyclopedist,
philosopher and above all biographer.
He is especially well known in this latter
capacity through his book Parallel Lives,
a collection of biographies of the most
famous men of the ancient world which
constitutes a major source of information
about Roman and Greek history.

ΤΟΥ ΝΙΚΑΝ ΚΡΕΙΤΤΟΝ
ΕΣΤΙ ΤΟ ΚΑΛΩΣ
ΧΡΗΣΘΑΙ ΤΗΣ ΝΙΚΗΣ

Better than victory
is its correct use.

ΣΤΑΓΟΝΕΣ ΥΔΑΤΟΣ
ΠΕΤΡΑΣ ΚΑΛΑΙΝΟΥΣΙΝ

Drops of water
can make holes in rock.

ΥΔΩΡ ΘΟΛΕΡΟΝ ΚΑΙ
ΨΥΧΗΝ ΑΠΑΙΔΕΥΤΟΝ
ΟΥΔΕΙΣ ΤΑΡΑΤΤΕΙΝ

Disturb neither muddy waters
nor uneducated minds.

ΜΗ ΠΑΙΔΙ ΜΑΧΑΙΡΑΝ
Η ΠΑΡΟΙΜΙΑ...
ΕΓΩ ΔΕ ΦΑΙΗΝ
ΑΝ ΜΗΔΕ ΑΝΔΡΙ
ΑΠΑΙΔΕΥΤΩ
ΔΥΝΑΣΤΕΙΑΝ

Do not give knives to children,
the proverb says. By the same
token, I'd say we should not give
power to an uneducated man.

ΤΑ ΧΑΛΕΠΑ ΤΑΙΣ
ΕΠΙΜΕΛΕΙΑΙΣ ΑΛΙΣΚΕΤΑΙ

Difficulties are overcome with thoroughness.

His life

The life of Plutarch is well known to us through his work. He was born and spent most of his life in Chaeronea in Boeotia, in the little town in which Philip of Macedon had defeated the allied forces of the Athenians, Thebans, Corinthians, and others.

His family was wealthy and aristocratic. As a young man he went to Athens to complete his studies, since it was still the city of philosophers. He apprenticed with the neo-Platonist Ammonius Saceas of Alexandria, who initiated him into all the philosophic systems. But his thirst for knowledge was unsatisfied, which was why he left Athens and went to Alexandria where there were significant institutions of higher learning and a fine library. There he supplemented his philosophic studies and attended classes in the physical sciences.

He also went on long voyages and, as was the custom at that time, spent a good deal of time in Rome, where he gave speeches on various moral issues. His inadequate command of Latin prevented him from learning as much as he wanted about Roman literature. Nevertheless he was able in Rome to consult documents and records that were useful to him in writing *Parallel Lives*. He became closely associated with famous Romans and his reputation was such that many dignitaries attended his classes and showed him their appreciation.

Plutarch lived his life in accordance with his moral theories. His fellow citizens honoured him with many offices which he assumed willingly, not to satisfy his ambition, but to serve his homeland better.

His work

The writings of Plutarch are significant, and can be divided into two groups the *Moralia* and *Parallel Lives*.

The *Moralia* consists of 83 essays, mainly of moral content, which cover many different topics, historical, religious, literary, etc. They are in the form of dialogues or diatribes and represent half of his extant work. The reader can obtain a general overview just by reading the titles of these treatises.

The other half of Plutarch's work is, as mentioned earlier, his *Parallel Lives*. This work has been widely read and has greatly influenced European thought and literature. It is one of our best sources of knowledge about Roman and Greek history: a collection of 50 biographies of famous men, Greeks and Romans. Forty-six of them consist of 23 pairs, each one containing the biography of one Greek and one Roman. At the end, they are compared and contrasted.

The biographies, in pairs, are of: Theseus-Romulus, Solon-Publicolas, Themistocles-Camillus, Aristidis-Marcus Kato, Cimon-Lucullus, Pericles-Fabius Maximus, Nicias-Crassus, Coriolanus-Alcibiades, Demosthenes-Cicero, Phocion-Cato, Dion-Brutus, Emilius Paulus-Timoleon, Septorius-Eumenes, Philopoemen-T. Flaminius, Pelopidas-Marcellus, Alexander-Caesar, Demetrius-Anthony, Pyrrhus-Marius, Aratus-Artaxerxes, Agis and Cleomenes-Tiberius and G. Gracchii, Lycurgus-Numa, Lysander-Sulla, Agesilaus-Pompey, Galba-Otho.

These biographies are not fiction or myth. They are real historic facts that Plutarch has drawn from many different sources. He studied all the authors who preceded him, and quotes names, works and information that we would not know today had it not been for him.

Those whose biographies he wrote cannot all be regarded as role models, such as Demetrius the Beseiger or Mark Anthony. But Plutarch decided also to write the life of persons whose example should be avoided, "as did the Spartans, who after getting the serfs drunk, put them in rooms used for group meals, to imbue the horror of drunkenness in young people".

Plutarch should not be regarded as a historian like Thucydides or Polybius. He is a famous dabbler in history and a biographer, but also a man with encyclopaedic knowledge and a philosopher. He was a widely read and religious intellectual who justified magic and all types of superstitions and agreed that the gods of the different peoples are not in fact different divinities, but the same divinity with the same powers, that have been given different names by each people.

Plutarch, whose aim was to delight and edify, wrote the only series of parallel biographies known in Western literature, and does not belong to any recognised category of authors, apart from that of the very erudite. His great learning, his admiration for the past and love of virtue often caused him to be regarded as the embodiment of Hellenism.

He is in fact, a unique figure in the history of Greek literature.

ΕΥΡΟΙΣ Δ'ΑΝ ΕΠΙΙΩΝ ΠΟΛΕΙΣ ΑΤΕΙΧΙΣΤΟΥΣ
ΑΓΡΑΜΜΑΤΟΥΣ ΑΒΑΣΙΛΩΤΟΥΣ ΑΧΡΗΜΑΤΟΥΣ...
ΑΝΙΕΡΟΥΣ ΔΕ ΠΟΛΕΙΣ ΚΑΙ ΑΘΕΟΥΣ ΟΥΔΕΙΣ
ΕΣΤΙΝ ΟΥΔ' ΕΣΤΑΙ ΓΕΓΟΝΟΣ ΘΕΑΤΗΣ

One can find cities without walls, illiterate, ungoverned, poor.
But cities without sanctuaries or gods do not exist,
nor will they ever exist.

POLYBIUS
c.202-122 BC

His life and work

He was from Megalopolis in Arcadia, the son of Lycortas, general of the Achaean Confederacy. To make himself familiar with the sites on which the events he related occurred, he travelled to Africa, Spain, Gaul and the Alps.

The eighteen years during which Polybius had to remain in Rome proved beneficial to him, especially since it was, in the opinion of Cicero, the golden age of the republic. He was awed by the discipline he found; the Roman virtues and Roman society were closer to his personality than that of Achaea at that time, which was being torn asunder by discord.

The life of Polybius, full of political, military, diplomatic and research activity, did not prevent him from creating a rich body of writings. They include his *Histories*, a youthful biography of *Philopoemenos*, *Tactics*, a history of the *Numantine War*, and a treatise on the habitability of the equatorial region.

His *Histories* consist of 40 books, only five of whichhave been preserved complete. He tells the story of the Romans and the Greeks between the years 220 and 146 BC, i.e. over a period of about 75 years. He himself took part in many of the events he describes. He enjoys drawing conclusions and moral lessons from these events, to be used in the future. In any event, the main idea of his *Histories* is that Rome owes her grandeur to its political system, which was an amalgam of monarchic, oligarchic and democratic elements. This was Polybius' main work, the work of a lifetime.

His other works must have been written in the early years of his career. They have unfortunately been lost, which is why we know virtually nothing about their content, other than what we can surmise from their titles.

The work of Polybius was regarded as important even in his own lifetime. It was a valuable source for Diodorus, Titus Livius and Plutarch. In addition, it constituted the starting point for other historians who wrote a continuation of Polybius, including Poseidonius and later Strabo. There has been a renewed appreciation of his work in modern times.

ARRIAN
95-175 AD

His life and work

Arrian is one of the many Greeks who played an important role in Roman administration and also distinguished himself as a writer. He was born in Nicomedia in Bithynia. As a young boy he was a pupil of the Stoic philosopher Epictetus whose teachings impressed him profoundly.

Arrian, whom we regard primarily as the historian of Alexander the Great, was famous among his contemporaries not as a historian but as a philosopher, and it is not clear when he began to see himself as a historian. His role model was Xenophon, from whom he borrowed the titles of some of his works. Thus he wrote *Treatises* and an *Encheiridion*, a manual of the teachings of Epictetus, as Xenophon wrote *Memorabilia*; and *Anabasis Alexandrou* as Xenophon wrote *Anabasis Cyrou*; he even divided his book into seven books as Xenophon had.

Other extant writings of Arrian are *On Hunting*, which reveals his early love of hunting, *Indica* and *Wandering the earth*, an important work, both geographical in nature. An early work of his entitled *Discourses* in 12 books contained detailed notes from the teachings of Epictetus.

His works *Tactica*, and *Wandering the earth* were based on notes from some of his service reports from the period when he served in the Roman army. Works by Arrian that have been lost include treatises on the subjects of *Bithynia*, *Parthia* and the *post-Alexandrine period* But the greatest of his works is *Anabasis Alexandrou*, which is the best of all ancient books about Alexander the Great. This book gives not only details about Alexander's campaign in Asia, but about all events from the moment he ascended the throne to his death.

Arrian had considerable abilities as a writer, but above all critical thought which is manifested with unrivalled success in his criticism of the sources he uses. Also, it was he who gave Greek traditions a valuable and creative role among the ranks of thoughtful Greeks and Romans, authors and intellectuals.

ΚΑΙ ΤΙ ΟΙΕΙ ΟΤΙ Ο ΗΡΑΚΛΗΣ Α ΑΠΕΒΗ
ΤΟΙΟΥΤΟΣ, ΕΙ ΜΗ ΛΕΩΝ ΟΥΤΟΣ ΕΓΕΝΕΤΟ...
Would Heracles have been the man he was,
had it not been for the lion (of Nemea)?

LUCIAN

c. 120-200 AD

His life and work

Satirist and pamphleteer born in Samosat, Syria. He wanted to become an orator, which was then the supreme goal of education. He learned his first letters in his native language of Aramaic, but later studied Greek language and rhetoric in western Asia Minor and became a lawyer in Antioch. He went on to study at various schools in Ionia, where he was taught Sophistic thought and rhetoric. Later he travelled to many places including Rome, where he was initiated into philosophy by the Platonist Nigrinus, and Gaul, where he made a living teaching rhetoric and reciting Sophist speeches. In 165 AD he moved to Athens and lived there for 20 years. During this time he wrote his philosophical and satirical dialogues and was highly esteemed for his penetrating thought, sparkling wit and caustic criticism. At an advanced age he accepted a high position in the courts of Alexandria, which was offered to him by the emperor Severus. He died in Alexandria.

More than 80 works are attributed to Lucian, some of which are spurious. The best known are his dialogues particularly the *Dialogues of the Gods* and the *Dialogues of the Dead*. In them he pokes fun at traditional mythology with some effort at moralising. *Tragic Zeus* and *Zeus Confuted* have the same purpose. Other works of his include *The Auction of Lives, Charon, Word-Flaunter, Teacher of Orators, Nigrinus, True History, Alexander* and *Banquet*.

Generally, the subjects of his writings are delightful because of their diversity. Lucian with his mordant wit penetrated the weaknesses of his contemporaries: the superstition, parasitism, and pretensions of wise men and philosophers, the vulgarity of the grammarians, and the arrogance of the powerful, which he excoriated with satiric banter and trenchant jests. A strong painter of human weakness, he satirises and mocks, not just to make the reader laugh, but to show the brilliant clarity and beauty of the Greek mind, in comparison to the semi-barbaric folly of his contemporaries.

His language is elegant and his style light. His splendid command of Greek served as a model for later writers.

ΤΟΝ ΤΩΝ ΔΑΝΑΪΔΩΝ ΠΙΘΟΝ
ΥΔΡΟΦΟΡΕΙΝ ΜΟΙ ΔΟΚΩ

I feel I am pouring water into the leaky jars of the Danaïds.

DIOGENEΣ LAERTIUΣ

3rd century AD

His life and work

He was from Laertes, a town in Cilicia, Asia Minor, and must have lived around the 3rd century AD. We know nothing about his life, other than what we can conclude from his work.

He wrote one sole book *Lives, Teachings and Sayings of Famous Philosophers,* which is divided into ten books and provides a panoramic view of Greek philosophy and thought from the period before him. It covers men such as Solon of Athens, poet and political reformer, and Periander of Corinth, neither of whom were primarily philosophers.

In his book, Diogenes Laertius includes 82 biographies of men from the 6th century to Epicurus who lived in the 4th. His work is in reality an attempt to write a history of philosophy and it is the only such history we have from antiquity

Although the author is not known for his writing talent or his critical mind, his work is nevertheless valuable for the information it contains. Diogenes undertakes a review of all the schools of philosophy and provides a brief biography of every philosopher from Thales to Epicurus, as well as a summary of their doctrines and a list of their works. Among other things, Diogenes preserved three letters of Epicurus. Apart from the history of philosophy, Diogenes Laertius quotes 49 of his own epigrams in the biographies of 43 philosophers. He also published a collection of *Epigrams*, in the first book of which he describes how some famous men died.

It can be seen from his work that Diogenes had received a sound education but we cannot conclude whether or not he had any particular knowledge of philosophy. His approach to philosophy is biographical and literary rather than philosophical. And it is virtually impossible to prove that Diogenes Laertius espoused any particular school of philosophy. The style of his work seems rather to indicate a man who happened to become interested in philosophers, but more as men and writers than for their philosophic work. The enormous value of Diogenes Laertius' *Lives* is due mainly to the fact that the sources he himself probably used have been lost, and that his work is the most important secondary source of information about the lives of ancient philosophers.

ΑΡΧΕ ΠΡΩΤΟΝ ΜΑΘΩΝ ΑΡΧΕΣΘΑΙ

Rule after first learning to be ruled.

The temple of Poseidon at Sounio was built between 444 and 440 BC.

INDEX OF NAMES

INDEX OF PHOTOGRAPHS

BIBLIOGRAPHY

The following works were used in the Greek language, either the original or in translation.

- *Ancient Greek Lyric Poets,* trans. K. Topouzis, Epikairotita.
- Aeschylus, *Agamemnon, Libation bearers, Eumenides,* Epikairotita.
- Yves Battistini, *Sappho,* Papadimas.
- A.S. Bogomolov, *History of Ancient Philosophy (Greece and Rome),* Eirmos.
- Andre Bonnard, *Ancient Greek Civilisation,* Themelio.
- Rita Boumi-Papa ed., *Maxims - Sayings,* G. Papakonstantinou.
- Robert Cohen, *Athenian Democracy,* Hermes.
- A. Constantinidis, *Dictionary of Proper Names: Mythological-Historical-Geographic,* Ekati.
- Luciano de Cresenzo, *History of Ancient Greek Philosophy,* 2 vols. Odysseas.
- Maurice Croisier, *The Civilisation of Ancient Greece,* Govostis.
- Pierre Ducasse, *The Great Philosophical Systems,* Everyman's Library.
- P.E. Easterling and B.M.W. Knox, *History of Ancient Greek Literature*
- D.N. Papadimas, *Education Issues,* Vol. V. *Synchroni Epochi.*
- Iason Evangelou, *Hellenic Civilisation,* Savvalas.
- *Excerpts from Pindar,* trans. K. Topouzis, Epikairotita.
- Robert Flacellere, *History of Ancient Greek Literature,* Papadimas.
- Egon Friedell, *Cultural History of Ancient Greece,* Poreia.
- A.Georgopapadakos, *Hellenic Letters,* Mochlos.
- K.D. Georgoulis. *History of Greek Philosophy.* Papadimas.
- Socrates Ghikas, *The Values of the Ancient Greeks.* Savvalas.
- S. Ghikas-I. Evangelou, *Pre-Socratic Philosophers,* Savvalas.
- Yannis Goudelis and Con. Spinos, *Theognis of Megara,* Nea Thesis.
- *History of the Greek Nation,* Ekdotiki Athenon.
- K.M. Kolombova-E.L.Ozeretskaya, *How the ancients lived,* Gnoseis.
- Yannis Kordatos, *History of Ancient Greek Philosophy,* Boukoumanis.
- *Diogenes Laertius,* Complete Works, Cactus.

- *Diogenes Laertius,* The Seven Wise Men of Antiquity, Paraskinio.
- Albin Lesky, *History of Ancient Greek Literature,* Kyriakidis.
- -Richard W. Livingstone, *Greek Ideals and Modern Life,* Pitsilos.
- Theophanis Manias, *The unknown achievements of the ancient Greeks,* Pyrinos Kosmos.
- *Menander the Difficult,* trans. K. Topouzis, Epikairotita.
- Robert J. Milch, *Homer's Odyssey,* Hermione.
- Claude Mosse, *The Ancient Creek Culture in the Enlightenment,* Savvalas.
- *The Myths of Aesop,* Ekphrasi.
- K.G. Papageorgiou, *Homer,* published by the author.
- G Papathanasopoulos, *Acropolis,* Krini.
- Plato, *Phaedrus,* Fexis.
- Plato, *Socrates' Defence.* Savvalas.
- Philostratos, *Complete Works,* Vol. IV, ™Life of the Sophists. Cactus.
- Gisella Richter, *Ancient Greek Art,* Kardamitsas.
- Jacqueline de Romilly, *Ancient Greek Letters,* Kardamitsas.
- N.M. Skouteropoulos, *Ancient Sophism,* Gnosi.
- Bruno Snell, *The discovery of the spirit,* National Bank of Greece Educational Foundation.
- Donald Strong, *World History of Art: The Classical World.* Fytrakis.
- B.T. Theodorakopoulos. *Introduction to Attic Rhetoric,* Epikairotita.
- Arnold Toynbee, *The Greeks and their legacy.* Kardamitsa.
- Volumes of the magazine *Archaeologia,* pub. Lambrakis Study Foundation
- W. Windelband-H. Heimsoeth, *Guide to the History of Philosophy,*
  National Bank of Greece Educational Foundation.
- Marguerite Yourcenar, *The Wreath and the Lyre.* Hatzinikolis.
- Zeller-Nestlem, *History of Greek Philosophy,* Estia Bookshop.
- Domi Encyclopedia.
- Epoptiki Encyclopedia.
- Great American Encyclopedia.
- Great Soviet Encyclopedia.
- Kosmos Encyclopedia.
- Papyrus-Larousse-Britannica Encyclopedia.

Texts: GEORGE PAPADOGEORGOS
Translator: JUDY GIANNAKOPOULOU
Publication - Text Editor: DAPHNE CHRISTOU
Artistic Editor: EVI DAMIRI

Production - Printing: M. Toubis S.A.